PRAISE FOR *IN THE BEDROOM*

Michael Wilmington

CHICAGO TRIBUNE

"In a way, *Killings* was Andre Dubus's answer to the classic, bare-bones Hemingway short story about murder in the everyday, *The Killers*—the classic that which Robert Siodmak and John Huston masterfully expanded into their famous 1946 film noir. Field performs similar magic here, sketching in what Dubus left out. Yet *In the Bedroom* is far less about violence than its causes and consequences. This film doesn't give us the shock and satisfaction of the usual movie morality play, because it's interested in something different: in truly exploring the moral and emotional dilemmas that people unexpectedly assaulted by horror undergo. It sneaks up on you and shakes you: a tale of the cold hell surging up beneath that windy, sensuous Wyeth landscape."

James Verniere

BOSTON HERALD

"How do civilized people bear a grief so unbearable it threatens to crush the civility on which their lives are founded? That may be the single most important question being asked of any of us these days, and it's certainly the most important issue addressed by any American movie. Todd Field's film does just that."

Roger Ebert

CHICAGO SUN-TIMES

"One of the best pictures of the year. Todd Field's *In the Bedroom* only slowly reveals its real subject in a story that has a shocking reversal at the end of the first act, and then looks more deeply than we could have guessed into the lives of its characters. Based on a story by the late Andre Dubus, the Massachusetts-based writer who died in 1999, and who worked with Field on the adaptation before his death. It works with indirection; the events on the screen are markers for secret events in the hearts of the characters, and the deepest insight is revealed, in a way, only in the last shot."

Chris Vognar

THE DALLAS MORNING NEWS

"The idea of an American heir to Ingmar Bergman may seem odd but one thing is for certain: A major filmmaking talent has arrived. Nearly every moment brings something to the narrative; it's a textbook study in how to tell a story through actions, not words, you'd be hard pressed to find a more economical film. *In the Bedroom* is a heart-wrenching film that gives you a lift through the sheer magic of its craft."

David Ansen

NEWSWEEK

"One of the best pictures of the year. Everything seems meticulously considered, conjuring up a hushed intimacy that instantly sucks you in. Todd Field exhibits a mastery of his craft many filmmakers never acquire in a lifetime."

Kenneth Turan

LOS ANGELES TIMES

"One of the best pictures of the year. An unadorned, unflinching film about the fierce and terrifying passions that can devastate a relationship. It pulls us in and does not let go. That restrained intensity, the film's inherent feeling tone, comes directly from the excellent 18-page short story by Andre Dubus that *In the Bedroom* is based on. The script, written by Field and Rob Festinger, smartly builds on that core, using Dubus' dialogue wherever possible and expanding the narrative to actually show us events that the short story only implied. Field has so completely merged with the material that it feels as if he became it and it became him. Each scene has its purpose and its weight, every image feels carefully thought out, every addition to the story—from moving it from Massachusetts to Field's home state of Maine to making use of the haunting, ethereal music of the Newark Balkan Girls Chorus of tiny Newark, Vt.—adds something of value."

John Anderson

NEWSDAY

"With an opening like Truffaut, a closing like Bergman and a sense of silence and subtlety, it was Field's precocious virtuosity with the intimate gesture, the small familiarity, the elasicity of space and time, that set this film apart. What *In the Bedroom* meant in 2001 were good things for the future of film. Field has a made a movie in which everything feels organic, nothing seems untrue and the effect is unforgettable."

Jack Mathews

NEW YORK DAILY NEWS

"One of the best pictures of the year. A remarkable achievement for Field, and a case study for other filmmakers who might agree that the power of drama comes through character, not action."

Lisa Schwarzbaum

ENTERTAINMENT WEEKLY

"Of the best pictures of the year. The big, breathtaking picture of unpredictable human action. This is a landscape Field understands and appreciates with the embrace of a real artist."

Peter Travers

ROLLING STONE

"One of the best films of the year. Todd Field makes a pitch-perfect feature filmmaking debut, and co-writes a script (with Rob Festinger) that resonates with ferocity and feeling."

IN THE BEDROOM

IN THE BEDROOM

A SCREENPLAY

Rob Festinger *and* Todd Field

Based on the short story *Killings*
by Andre Dubus

talk miramax books

HYPERION

NEW YORK

ISBN: 1-4013-5924-8

10 9 8 7 6 5 4 3 2 1

IN THE BEDROOM

Screenplay

by

Rob Festinger and Todd Field

Based Upon the Short Story

KILLINGS

by

Andre Dubus

FADE IN:

THE SOUND OF WIND AND NOTHING ELSE

EXT. GINN'S POINT - DAY

We are in the midst of a field of tall grass & wild flowers.

A long rutted road stretches into the distance. Faintly at first and then closer - we hear a woman squealing with laughter. We see her legs cut through the grass and fly up a hill. Close on her heels is a young man, a good ten years younger, in hot pursuit.

Over the field - across the tops of blades, sits an ancient apple tree. We rise out of the grass and see the two young people under the tree. They are entwined - in a deep embrace.

CLOSER NOW

We see them in glimpses:

Their eyes - Lips - Hands -

Finally they part - the woman rests her head on his chest.

She reaches out and strokes his hand.

He stares at their fingers mingling together.

The woman sighs.

                    WOMAN
          I Love it here.

                    MAN
          I know you do...

                    WOMAN
          I can feel my life - ya know.

He stares up into the boughs above him and smiles.

A legend appears: **IN THE BEDROOM**

THE SOUND OF A BALLGAME OVER:

EXT. RURAL ROUTE 90 - PREDAWN

A BLUE 1973 CHEVY PICK-UP winds around a corner and disappears down a long stretch of road. "And that's it from Fenway, the final score Oakland 3 the Redsox 7. You have been listening to the re-broadcast of last night's game. This broadcast is the sole property of Major League Baseball and cannot be-"

EXT. EMERSON ROAD - SAME

The truck pulls onto a small road flanked by rows of 100-year-old clapboard two-story affairs.

EXT. NATALIE'S HOUSE - SAME

Standing on the lawn in front of one of them, is the woman from
the opening scene, NATALIE STROUT, pretty - beautiful actually
with a little more sleep. She stands with two small boys who
are doing their best to stay warm in the morning air. Her son
JASON 8, and his brother DUNCAN 4, who has his face buried in
his mother's coat--refusing to see or be seen.

The truck comes to a stop and two men get out. One is young,
early 20's, and even at this hour his step is lively, his
face full of warmth. He walks over to Natalie and gives her a
kiss. The young man from the opening scene, FRANK FOWLER.The
other man leans back against the passenger door. He is in
his early 50's. Kind face, good looking, athletic in his day -
Frank's father, MATT. He smiles at Natalie.

Natalie smiles back.

                    NATALIE
          Morn'in Dr. Fowler.

                    MATT
          Morn'in Natalie. How you doing boys?

                    JASON
          Great!

Jason starts for the truck. Matt opens the door and the boy
climbs inside the cab.

Frank kneels down to Duncan.

                    FRANK
          Hey buddy...you upset that you're not
          coming?

Frank reaches out and puts his hand on the boy's shoulder.
Duncan pulls away.

Frank looks up to Natalie for help.

                    FRANK
          He can come if he wants...we can manage,
          really.

 She smiles and shakes her head.

                    NATALIE
          Go ahead. He wants to stay here.

                    FRANK
          Don't worry Dunk. You can come next time.

Natalie kisses him and they're off.

INT. TRUCK - SAME - MOVING

Jason in the middle. He glances over to Frank - a trace of
hero worship in his face.

INT. STROUT & SONS CANNERY - DAWN

Sardines are processed at lightening speed. We follow them on their journey, which ends with the sealed cans being packed into cardboard shipping boxes. They are taped shut by a young man we will meet later (TIM Bryson, 30). The tops read STROUT & SONS.

INT. ATKINS LOBSTER CO-OP - DAWN

A double-55-gallon-drum wood stove is humping. Several men turn their bodies rotisserie-fashion around the thing, while making morning small talk - The starting price of lobsters, the prospect of repairs to their equipment, and so on.

A SCARRED HAND scribbles some figures on a wall that has been used as a scratch pad for years.

Two scales are emptied of RED FISH into a PLASTIC PICKLE BUCKET.

EXT. HARBOR - SAME

A pair of CANVAS TENNIS SHOES shuffle down a gangway. The bucket sways directly over them. A small hand struggles with the weight of the thing. A pair of BEACON FALLS waders appear - the shoes stop. A strong hand grabs hold of the handle - the shoes pick up the pace.

EXT. HARBOR - SAME

Matt & Frank prepare the rig.

Jason stands on the dock, taking it all in. A field of LOBSTER POTS stacked like cordwood and surrounded by a collection of SCARRED BUOYS, GRAPNEL and coiled FISHING GEAR stiff with sea salt - all so wildly unreasonable as to seem exotic.

Jason's eyes find the hull of "GIGI" an old Boudreau built lobsterboat. Starboard side covered in barnacles.

                    FRANK
          C'mon up Jace.

                    MATT
          Hold on a second. Need to know if he's
          ready first - Jason, can you tell me
          what's important?

Jason hesitates.

                    FRANK
          Go on tell him.

                    JASON
               (nervous)
          "A shaft of sunlight at the end of a dark
          afternoon, a note in music--

He takes a breath.

>   JASON
>   -and the way the back of a baby's neck
>   smells if its mother keeps it tidy."

>   MATT
>   (to Frank)
>   You taught him well.

Jason beams.

>   MATT
>   - Come aboard sailor.

Matt reaches down to give a hand up.

Frank turns the engine over. It roars to life.

EXT. HARBOR - LATER

The sun is fast climbing into the morning sky as "GIGI"
glides out of the channel and past a LIGHTHOUSE that sits
just off the point of a good sized ISLAND.

Jason shields his eyes with his hand. He gazes out at the
island. Matt comes up beside him and sticks a baseball cap
onto his head. The crown reads U.S.S. CONSTELLATION.

>   JASON
>   Thank you.

>   MATT
>   Ever been over there?

>   JASON
>   No sir.

>   MATT
>   It's beautiful. Isn't an island anymore
>   though. It's a city. They have electric
>   lights. Artesian wells, even a jail -
>   lighthouse isn't manned anymore - it's
>   run by a computer - When I lived there,
>   had no ferry then, so we didn't even have
>   cars, can you believe that?

>   JASON
>   How'd you get back?

>   MATT
>   Off the island?

Jason nods.

>   MATT
>   We rowed.

Matt smiles at the memory.

                    MATT
          Then we got a little outboard. That was
          great. A seven and a half horsepower it
          was - we lived there until I was about
          your age - then we left and became
          "harbor people."

Jason seems to be digesting this.

                    JASON
          Am I a "harbor person"?

Matt hides a smile about to form.

                    MATT
          Yep, Jason - we all are.

Jason is full of questions. Matt knows the answers and
doesn't talk down to him. Something the boy is grateful for.

FRANK

At the helm. His eyes squinted from glare and cold. He cuts
back on the throttle and heads for the winch.

GLOVED HANDS pull up a BLUE-GREEN BUOY and slide the MANILA
LINE into the WINCH.

A POT surfaces and Frank sets it "Doors up" on the edge. He
opens the doors. His hands work quickly and efficiently. He
tosses a SMALL CRAB back into the water, pulls out a LOBSTER
and measures the back. Too small. Then a nice sized LOBSTER
is pulled out - it's missing the SCISSOR CLAW. He hands it to
Matt. Baits the trap. Throws the winch and the next pot
surfaces.

HELM

Matt sits inside, Jason on his lap. He reaches into a WOODEN
BOX of RUBBER BANDS with a BANDING WRENCH and bands the
crustacean's remaining CRUNCHER CLAW.

Jason stares at the disfigured creature.

                    MATT
          Oh boy...now you see what happened to
          this poor fellow?

                    JASON
          ...what?

                    MATT
          Well, the trap has nylon nets called
          heads--2 side heads at both ends, so the
          lobster can crawl in. The "Bedroom" head
          inside, holds the bait and keeps it from
          escaping--you know the old saying "two's
          company three's a crowd"?

Jason nods.

> MATT
> Well, it's like that. You get more than
> two in a *bedroom* and chances are -
> something like *this* is going to happen.
> That's why Frank can't leave these traps
> for more than a day-

Matt holds up another Lobster and turns it belly-up. There
are black balls on both sides of the tail.

> MATT
> Now the older females like this ol gal,
> are the most dangerous - especially when
> they're growin' berries.

> JASON
> Berries?

> MATT
> Eggs....one of these can take out two
> males easy - Then you wind up with
> lobster you can't sell - and as for this
> fine lady, she gets off easy, the state
> says you have to let her go.

Matt throws her back into the water. Holds up the other one to Jason.

> MATT
> Can you handle this?

Jason nods.

> MATT
> (Gently)
> You sure?

He really isn't. Matt hands it to him.

> MATT
> Go ahead now, put it in the tank.

Jason can't get the thing in the tank fast enough.

EXT. FOWLER HOUSE - DAY

Looking around, you see a big yard, double lot. The grass is
manicured to perfection, someone takes a lot of pride in
their garden. In the middle of this sits a two story cape,
post Hopper/Wyeth, early 20th Century - simple, beautiful,
and you don't freeze in the winter.

The truck backs up into the driveway, Frank jumps out, drops
the gate. Resting on the bed is a LARGE BOX with a line drawing
of a SWING-SET.

> FRANK O.S.
> Hey, dad can you give me a hand?

The transistorized sounds of a baseball game.

EXT. FOWLER - BACKYARD - LATER

Frank pushes Duncan, who sits proudly on his new swing-set.

                    DUNCAN
          Higher! HIGHER!

SMALL CHILDREN are everywhere. A serious Super Soaker Squirt Gun fight in progress.

ACROSS THE YARD

a steaming hot grill, with a huge assortment of hot-dogs & burgers. A spatula flips a patty.

The sounds of Fenway park emanate from a cheap portable radio.

WILLIS GRINNEL, early 50's, a stout, silver-haired man, works the grill. Standing next to him is Matt, his best friend for forty plus years.

Matt takes a pull off a can of Moxie. Sets it down and searches through a plastic bread bag.

Willis looks past him, distracted.

                    MATT
          Ahh, Ruth hates this kind.

                    WILLIS
          What?

                    MATT
          I bought the wrong buns.

                    WILLIS
          Maybe we can borrow hers.

Matt follows Willis's gaze, to the object of his distraction:

A PRETTY WOMAN IN TIGHT DENIM SHORTS. She's bent over to wipe the ketchup-stained face of Jason (he's wearing Matt's cap).

                    WILLIS
          Ah, what I would give to have back my
          youth.

                    MATT
          Willis, you never had that in your youth.

The woman turns around and catches Willis staring. It's Natalie.

Willis looks down, nonchalantly rifling through the bun bag.

Matt waves to a passing man in khaki shorts, FATHER OBERTI, 50's.

                         MATT
              Father! You made it!

                         FATHER OBERTI
              Hey, if I don't see you fellas here, I
              don't get to see you at all.

ON FRANK

He backwards-hugs Natalie.

                         FRANK
              You want a beer?

                         NATALIE
              I think I'll see if your Mom needs any
              help.

                         FRANK
              Good luck.

She laughs. He grabs and tickles her but she breaks away and
escapes inside the house.

Matt watches on, and falls into a wistful daydream.

                         WILLIS
              Jealous?

Matt turns to him and, to Willis's surprise, ever so slightly,
nods.

INT. FOWLER HOUSE - LIVING ROOM - SAME

Natalie walks in through the living room, pausing to examine
a half finished ARCHITECTURAL MODEL that sits on a card-table
next to a jigsaw puzzle.

She looks toward the kitchen where a woman works at the sink.
She takes a breath and starts there.

INT. FOWLER GARAGE - DAY

REAR OF THE GARAGE

Frank reaches into an old Westinghouse refrigerator. He pulls
out a case of Schaeffer's and a six-pack of Moxie. He loads it
all into a metal tub filled with ice.

                         VOICE O.S.

              Yo.

Frank, hunched over as he works, looks up at

FRONT OF THE GARAGE

Tim Bryson still in his work clothes: He wears a white soiled
smock. A patch on his right pocket says STROUT & SONS. Over the
left simply TIM. A hair-net nests on his head.

                    FRANK
          Thanks for coming by. Wooo, is that new
          cologne? You really oughta take a shower
          when you leave that place.

                    TIM
          Very funny.

                    FRANK
          Take off that head dress, chief, and give
          me a hand?

Tim reaches up and pulls the hair-net off his head.

EXT. FOWLER HOUSE - DAY

SIDE OF THE HOUSE

Tim and Frank lug the heavy cooler around the house, heading
toward the backyard.

                    TIM
          So, Mr. Strout mentioned you again.

                    FRANK
          I bet he did.

                    TIM
          Seriously, man. He still talks about you
          coming back. Says you're the best can
          packer he ever had.

Tim and Frank emerge from the side of the house. Willis cuts
them off, grabs two beers.

                    WILLIS
          Excuse me boys - an offering. Catch
          Father.

He throws one to Father Oberti, who sits talking with Willis's wife,
KATIE GRINNEL 50's, she is talking the priest's ear off.

                    KATIE
          Becky went to the hairdressing academy
          after high school, but after she got
          married and had the boys, she decided she
          wanted to stay home - she still loves
          doing hair though. Where do you go
          Father?

                    FATHER OBERTI
          I just go to Super Cuts.

                    KATIE
          You can't request the same girl at Super
          Cuts - you have to take what you can get.
          They don't know your hair - how can you
          get a good cut if they don't know the
          hair?

Father Oberti has the patience of...well,of a priest.

INT. FOWLER HOUSE - DAY

RUTH FOWLER 50, attractive, is washing and arranging
vegetables on a plate. Natalie chops carrots on a cutting
board.

They barely make eye-contact. Natalie attempts small talk.

                    RUTH
          Can you hand me that bowl dear?

She does.

                    RUTH
          Thank you.

                    NATALIE
          I'm looking forward to the concert on
          Labor day. The music is so...unusual -
          haunting really.

Ruth keeps chopping. Natalie chooses her words carefully.

                    NATALIE
          How did you learn about that particular
          style?

                    RUTH
          At Brown...my thesis was on Eastern
          European folk music.

Natalie's lips tighten uncomfortably. The topic seems to intimidate.

                    NATALIE
              (lightly)
          I thought of becoming a teacher.

                    RUTH
          Why didn't you?

The answer to Ruth's question (Duncan) wanders in. His cheeks
as big as Dizzy Gillespie's.

                    NATALIE
          What are you eating?

Duncan's mouth is so full he can hardly speak.

                    DUNCAN
          ...nothing.

The two regard each other

                    NATALIE
          How is it?

                    DUNCAN
               (Smiling)
          Good.

He tugs on her shirt.

                    DUNCAN
          Swing me, Swing me.

                    NATALIE
          Okay, okay Dunk...

She gets dragged out of the kitchen. The screen door slams.

Ruth finishes arranging the plate. Matt enters, and starts opening up the cupboards looking for something.

He squats down, burrowing into a cabinet.

                    MATT
          It was nice of you to invite the boys.

                    RUTH
          She hasn't brought them before because
          she's embarrassed. She shouldn't be
          embarrassed.

Matt looks up from the floor.

                    MATT
               (to Ruth)
          Nice view from down here.

She ignores him, but smiles.

EXT. FOWLER BACKYARD - DAY

FRANKis hunched over, with his arms gently wrapped around Jason, coaching him on the finer points of hitting. Tim pitches.

                    FRANK
          There you go ... good, hands up, higher.
          That's it. Bend your knees -

THE SWING-SET

Duncan is being pushed by Natalie, Ruth, watches from the kitchen window.

INT. FOWLER HOUSE - DAY

MATCH CUT: Ruth, staring out the window.

>   RUTH
>   I don't know why you had to put that
>   monstrosity up. You're just going to have
>   to take it apart when they leave.

Matt rises, a bottle of lighter fluid in hand.

>   MATT
>   C'mon, Ruth, he's a kid. What did you
>   expect? "Happy Birthday, here's a box.
>   Why don't you drag it around for a while?"
>   He's a kid. He wants it now.

Something across the yard catches her attention.

>   RUTH
>   Oh, great.

EXT. FOWLER HOUSE - DAY

Matt exits the house.

ACROSS THE YARD

Duncan jumps off his swing and sprints.

TO RICHARD

who has just arrived. He stays at the far end of the yard.
Duncan does a running jump into his father's arms.

>   DUNCAN
>   Daddy!

Frank with Jason, looks up.

Jason sees his father. He doesn't move.

Natalie walks over to Frank, they exchange glances.

>   NATALIE
>   C'mon Jason.

>   JASON
>   No.

>   NATALIE
>   Now.

She grabs his hand. Straining to appear casual, traverses the
yard to

RICHARD AND DUNCAN.

Richard play-boxes Duncan.

Duncan looks up at his mother.

>   DUNCAN
>   Daddy's taking us to the arcade.

Richard, eating Duncan's hot dog, rises to meet Natalie and Jason.

                    RICHARD
          Hey there buddy...Come on over here Jace.

Jason looks away.

                    DUNCAN
               (To Jason)
          I told you he'd come - buttface.

Jason reaches over and whacks Duncan on the head.

                    RICHARD
               (angry)
          Hey Jason - Don't do that to your
          brother. You want me to do that to you?

He probably has. Jason backs away.

Frank makes his way over to Natalie.

AT THE GRILL

Matt watches on, absently flipping burgers.

Ruth comes over to him.

                    RUTH
          Matt ...

                    MATT
          It's ok.

Ruth shakes her head.

Richard, Frank and Natalie are talking, but there are long pauses between words. Tim wanders over and says something to Richard.

Finally, Richard smiles, turns, and exits. Alone.

Jason playfully chases Duncan across the yard.

Frank and Natalie stay behind, talking quietly.

Matt takes a breath, and exhales. He turns to Ruth with a comforting smile, but

she's just entering the house. The screen door closes behind her.

INT. FOWLER HOUSE - KITCHEN - SAME

Ruth is at the counter pouring dressing onto a salad. Frank comes up behind her and hugs her.

                    FRANK
          Thanks for doing this, Mom.

                    RUTH
          Are you alright?

                    FRANK
          Sure. Natalie and I want to take you and
          dad out tonight.

                    RUTH
          Oh that's very sweet dear, but we already
          have plans.

                    FRANK
          You going over to the Grinnel's?

Ruth shakes her head.

                    RUTH
               (smiles)
          Your father's taking me to the Strand.

                    FRANK
          Oh, what are you seeing?

                    RUTH
          Oh, I don't know - but he says it's the
          first film we ever saw together.

THE SOUND OF PISTOL FIRE.

INT. STRAND THEATER - NIGHT

Matt & Ruth sit watching BARRY LYNDON. The duel between Barry &
Lord Bullingdon is on screen. Bullingdon's pistol misfires.

                    LORD BULLINGDON
          Sir Richard this pistol must be faulty -
          I must have another.

                    AIDE TO RICHARD
          I'm sorry Lord Bullingdon but you must
          first stand your ground and allow Mr.
          Lyndon his turn to fire.

                    SIR RICHARD
          That is correct Lord Bullingdon - your
          pistol has fired and that counts as your
          shot--Mr. Lyndon are the rules of firing
          clear to you?

                    BARRY
          - yes -

                    SIR RICHARD
          Lord Bullingdon are you ready to receive
          Mr. Lyndon's fire?

                    LORD BULLINGDON
          ...yes -

                        SIR RICHARD
          Very well then - Mr. Lyndon cock your
          pistol and prepare to fire.

Bullingdon is overwrought. He looks like he may vomit.

Ruth leans over to Matt.

                        RUTH
          Let's go.

Ruth gets out of her seat. Matt looking confused follows.

EXT. STRAND THEATRE - SAME

Ruth heads out the doors with Matt on her heels.

                        MATT
          What's wrong?

                        RUTH
          I don't remember it being so tragic.

                        MATT
          Oh...I always felt sorry for Barry.

                        RUTH
          Please.

                        MATT
          No, I mean it - maybe I relate to him.

                        RUTH
          What *are you* talking about?

                        MATT
          Well, we both married above our station.

                        RUTH
          Don't start that again.

A moment. He takes her in his arms and kisses her. Looks into
her eyes.

                        MATT
          Happy anniversary.

                        RUTH
               (smiles)
          Happy anniversary.

He buries his face in her hair.

          MATT   RUTH
I love you.   - I know -

INT. FOWLER HOUSE - BEDROOM - NIGHT

Ruth sits at her bureau facing the mirror. She begins a nightly ritual of removing the pins from her hair once made from the shells of tortoises and now the plastics of Dupont.

Matt lies in bed reading. He lowers his book and watches her brush her tresses with long, delicious strokes. She sets down her brush and turns. Matt looks back to his book.

She climbs into bed next to him.

                    RUTH
          She's not divorced yet.

                    MATT
          It's the same thing. Maine has crazy
          laws, that's all...he likes the boys.

                    RUTH
          You don't think he's thinking about-

                    MATT
          No...he's not going to marry her.

                    RUTH
          Then what's he doing with her?

                    MATT
          She probably loves him, Ruth. Girls
          always have. Why can't we just leave it
          at that?

                    RUTH
          Hmmmm. He won't listen to me. I asked him
          three times to dismantle that swing-set.

                    MATT
          Oh, let it stay up. Looks like a young
          couple lives here.

                    RUTH
          He needs his head in school. Not in her.

                    MATT
          So to speak.

Ruth pinches his shoulder.

                    MATT
          Oww!

                    RUTH
          It would help if you were on my side.

                    MATT
               (playfully)
          I'll get on your side.

She laughs and pushes him away.

INT. UNION CLINIC - WAITING ROOM - DAY

A small waiting room with an alcove reception. ROCKWELL PRINTS
adorn the walls, a long table covered with dog-eared periodicals,
rests in front of a couch that has seen better days.

ALMA ADAMSON 80's, glances over at her husband, ELWYN 80's, who
vacantly thumbs through a HIGHLIGHTS MAGAZINE. He pauses to
catch-up on the latest exploits of GOOFUS & GALLANT.

The nurse, JANELLE 40's, calls out from the alcove.

                    JANELLE O.S.
          Mr. and Mrs. Adamson?

INT. UNION CLINIC - EXAMINATION ROOM

Elwyn sits bare chested on a table. Matt finishes bandaging his
elbow - then listens to his chest with a stethoscope. He is
careful and thoughtful. Alma looks to him. Worried.

                    MATT
          You can put your shirt back on now.

Alma stands and helps her husband dress.

                    ALMA
          Yesterday he was up and around all
          afternoon, but today - he tumbled. He's
          fallen down twice. I have all I can do to
          get him up. He's weak and the longer you
          lay in bed - the weaker you get.

                    MATT
          Elwyn, you need to do those exercises,
          you promised me, twice a day.
          I know you miss the work - but it's
          important.

                    ALMA
              (to Matt)
          Man didn't have ache nor pain--he's just
          gave up...said when he couldn't work no
          more, he didn't want to live. For a while
          he'd sit and just mend on nets - but he
          can't do that anymore.

                    ELWYN
              (speaks with difficulty)
          How's your dad Matt?

                    ALMA
          I'm sorry Dr. - now Elwyn you remember
          Jesse Fowler passed on sometime back, we
          were at the funeral. Remember?

Elwyn nods.

Matt knows. He's heard this before. Sometimes he feels more like a mechanic than a doctor, working on old cars with parts that have long been discontinued. He nods sympathetically.

INT. MATT'S OFFICE - HALLWAY - LATER

Matt pulls on his jacket. He passes Janelle in the hallway as he heads for the back door.

                    MATT
          I'll be back in an hour. Forgot my lunch.

                    JANELLE
          Starting to become a habit. I can get you
          something from Willis's.

He's already out the door.

EXT. HARBOR - SAME

Matt trots down the gangway and up to where the "GIGI" is moored. He looks in. No sign of Frank. A VOICE BOOMS from a new 35ft. JONESPORTER - it belongs to HENRY OZAR 50's.

                    HENRY
          Just missed him Matt, he went home for
          lunch today.

                    MATT
          Right...I forgot he's got that interview.

INT. FOWLER HOUSE - DAY

Matt enters. Looks around. Calls up the stairs.

                    MATT
          Frank? Frank? Hello?

                    FRANK O.S.
          Dad.

Matt turns around, and sees Frank.

                    MATT
          Frank? ... What are you doing? Thought you
          were driving to Boston for that
          interview?

Frank slowly nods. His clothes are rumpled.

                    FRANK
          yeah - he - we rescheduled.

                    MATT
               (knowing)
          uh huh.

NATALIE - walks out, from a room in the hall. She combs her
hair through with her fingers, but her skirt, on backward, is
somewhat of a giveaway.

Frank rolls his eyes.

>   NATALIE
>   Hello, Dr. Fowler.
>
>   MATT
>   Hi, where are the boys?
>
>   NATALIE
>   (sheepishly)
>   ...with my mom.

Then.

>   MATT
>   (to Natalie)
>   Oh...Like coleslaw?

THE KITCHEN TABLE

Matt sits across from Natalie and Frank. Sandwiches, iced tea
and coleslaw are laid out.

Frank looks to Matt for some kind of acknowledgment of his
lunch-time activities. Matt seems more interested in the slaw.

EXT. ELK'S FIELD - DAY

BLEACHERS

Frank is sandwiched between Matt and Ruth. They are surrounded
by dozens of young parents.

Ruth doesn't look too thrilled to be here.

>   FRANK
>   Wave you guys.

Matt and Ruth follows Frank's gaze, to:

DOWN BELOW

Natalie has her hands full adjusting Jason's uniform while
Duncan clings to her. She is waving up to the Fowlers amidst
the chaos.

THE BLEACHERS.

The Fowlers wave back.

Matt's suddenly inspired. He leans in past Ruth, to Frank.

>   MATT
>   Did you tell your Mom how good it was?

                    RUTH
          How good what was?

                    MATT
          Frank had quite a time this afternoon –
          loved your coleslaw. Ate enough for two.

                    RUTH
          That's what it's there for...

Frank leans back behind Ruth to give his father the evil eye.

He gets a grin from Matt for his trouble. Ruth almost catches
it.

Matt rises, shuffles past Ruth and Frank, whom he gives a firm
pat on the knee.

                    MATT
          Hot dogs?

                    FRANK
          I'll take one.

Ruth puts her arm around Frank.

                    RUTH
              (re: Duncan and Jason)
          So, how are the kids?

Frank's caught off-guard. He shakes his head.

                    RUTH
          ... things okay?

                    FRANK
          Fine.

                    RUTH
          Good, good.

Then.

                    RUTH
          How'd your interview go?

                    FRANK
              (too fast)
          Great.

                    RUTH
          Oh, good.

Ruth watches Natalie below.

                    RUTH
          She's such a *brave* girl.

                        FRANK
          That's it. You're driving me nuts, Ma.
          Really. I've had lots of girlfriends.

                        FRANK
          I don't understand why this one is any
          different.

                     RUTH
          I know you don't.

                        FRANK
          We're not serious, Mom.

                        RUTH
          No?

                        FRANK
          No. It's a summer thing.

She would like to believe him.

                        RUTH
          I see.

INT. NATALIE'S CAR - DAY

Natalie drives down Emerson Road.

As she approaches her house, she sees a brown Suburban sitting
in her driveway. She looks confused.

INT. NATALIE'S HOUSE - DAY

THE KITCHEN

Natalie enters with groceries.

Richard is seated at the kitchen table. He's finishing the first half
of a sandwich. He drains a glass of milk.

Natalie sets her purse down on the counter, and starts cleaning
up his mess.

                        NATALIE
          How'd you get in this time?

                        RICHARD
                  (playing along)
          Chimney.

She takes the carton of milk that Richard, no doubt, left out. She pours
the final drops into his glass.

                        RICHARD
          Thank you.

She throws the carton out. She takes a seat, and stares at him
like a teacher counselling a troubled youth.

                          NATALIE
              What can I help you with?

He kicks back the last of the milk, wipes his mouth.

                          RICHARD
              I was just dropping that off for Jason.

                          NATALIE
              What?

                          RICHARD
              That.

He points to a BASEBALL TROPHY sitting on top of the microwave.
An inscription bears his name and "Rockland High School 1982
Regional Championship."

                          RICHARD
              I didn't know where you'd want to put it.
              It was about time he got it. What am I
              going to do with it?

Richard's wistful gaze stays locked on the trophy.

For a moment, Natalie's guard slips away.

                          NATALIE
              I think it will mean a lot to him,
              Richard. He's really been improving
              lately ...

                          RICHARD
                   (a sharp turn)
              So I've heard.

                          NATALIE
              It would have been nice if you'd come to
              his game.

                          RICHARD
              I just got your message. Where are they,
              with *him*?

                          NATALIE
              That's none of your business.

                          RICHARD
              I see. They're my kids but they're none of
              my business.

                          NATALIE
              You know what I mean.

Richard presses his fingers to his eyes. He takes a long, heavy
breath.

                          RICHARD
              I ... I was thinking about moving back.
              Here. With you and the boys.

                    NATALIE
          What are you talking about?

                    RICHARD
          What am I talking about? I'm talking about
          moving back, that's what I'm talking
          about - I know what you're thinking, but
          it's different now.

                    NATALIE
          Oh, really? How's the job? Your father
          take you back on at the cannery?

                    RICHARD
               (dryly)
          That's funny. You're still getting checks
          aren't you?

She ignores him

                    RICHARD
          Ya see my new rig out there?

Natalie looks annoyed.

                    NATALIE
          Yeah - it's real nice.

                    RICHARD
          It's not exactly new, I traded David the truck
          for it. It's got room for all of us - a good
          grocery gettin car.

A moment.

                    RICHARD
          You wantta take a ride?

                    NATALIE
               (laughing)
          Jesus, Richard, you don't change, do you?

                    RICHARD
          Change? No, I don't change. Everything
          around me changes. You change. You take my
          house, you take my kids, you fuck this
          other guy. No, I don't change at all.

                    NATALIE
          It's not your house.

                    RICHARD
          Oh. No?

                    NATALIE
          No. And as far as *fucking* goes ...who was it
          that answered your phone the other morning?

                    RICHARD
          She...

                         NATALIE
          I don't care. Really, you can just stop
          now. It's not working.

He takes a breath.

                         RICHARD
          I just want...a chance.

                         NATALIE
          For what? To fool them for a few days into
          thinking they have a real father, and then
          it's back to -

                         RICHARD
                    (cutting her off)
          I am their father.

                         NATALIE
                    (vehement)
          No, Richard. You know what defines a
          father? It's what he does, not what he
          promises. It's being a positive,
          consistent presence.

Richard eyes her suspiciously.

                         RICHARD
                    (mimicking her)
          "Positive consistent presence." *Wow*. What
          does that mean? I just don't get it. But
          I'm not fucking a college boy, am I?

                         NATALIE
          Look...can you just go now? I really don't
          want you here when they get back.

                         RICHARD
          Oh, no, wouldn't want _that._

He doesn't budge.

                         NATALIE
          You have to leave.

Finally, as if struck by some small discovery. Richard places
his large hands on the kitchen table and pushes himself up.

He heads past Natalie without looking back. He closes the door
firmly behind him.

EXT. NATALIE'S HOUSE - FRONT YARD - DUSK

Frank's truck parked out front.

The lawn is littered with the boy's various plastic weapons and
a small wading pool.

A children's television show is heard from inside.

Natalie is sprawled out on a chaise lounge, nursing a beer, and sharing a cigarette with Frank, who is on his hands & knees finishing an elaborate structure with a set of FROEBEL wooden blocks.

                    NATALIE
          You know I've been ignoring our
          difference in age, but if you keep
          playing with those blocks, I'm gonna
          start to worry.

                    FRANK
          They're not blocks - they're gifts.

                    NATALIE
          I'm sorry I know they're a gift and a
          very generous one. I'm just concerned
          that Dunk. might think he's a little old
          to be playing with them.

                    FRANK
          They're not for playing - they're to learn about
          unity & balance. Froebel called them "Gifts."
          This is the second gift - a sphere, a cube, and a
          cylinder. A five year old can learn the
          difference in form depending on how they look at
          them.

Why didn't he say so in the first place?

                    NATALIE
          Oh...you said second gift. How many are
          are there?

                    FRANK
          Twenty.

A moment.

                    NATALIE
          You've been playing with these - excuse
          me, working with these for how long?

                    FRANK
          Since I was about Dunk's age. My mom took
          me through all twenty.

So that's what a good mother does.

                    NATALIE
          ...oh.

                    FRANK
          Come on down here and take a look.

She sets down her beer and joins him. The small wooden structure looks like a home that could have been built by Lautner or Wright. Frank looks pleased. Natalie is distracted.

                    NATALIE
          Your Mother gave you these Frank - I feel
          funny Duncan having them.

                    FRANK
          Don't be silly, it was her idea.

                    NATALIE
               (skeptical)
          Really?

                    FRANK
          You're not looking at the house - look.
          It's not all mine, it's part Mack.

Frank speaks excitedly, as he makes a quick sketch on a colored
piece of construction paper using one of the boys' markers.

                    FRANK
          See the whole ideal of what Mack was
          trying to achieve was a common area in the
          middle of the house. I mean - a large,
          common space wasn't unique to Mack, but
          the idea of separating the family so that
          the kids were on one side and the parents
          on the other, so they would all spill into
          the center ...

He looks over to Natalie, checking in.

She smiles, and shifts her gaze.

                    FRANK
          I'm boring you, aren't I?

                    NATALIE
               (softly)
          No, not at all, I was just....just
          thinking.

                    FRANK
          About what?

                    NATALIE
          About you...school.

                    FRANK
          I'd rather talk about our house.

                    NATALIE
          I know you would.

                    FRANK
          What if I wait a year?

                    NATALIE
          Frank-

                    FRANK
          A year's not going to make a difference.

                    NATALIE
          You can't do that, Frank.

                    FRANK
          I've thought a lot about this.

                    NATALIE
          But you told me it takes forever just to
          establish yourself.

                    FRANK
          Exactly, so what's a year in forever?
          Know what Duncan said today?

She can't suppress a smile.

                    NATALIE
          You wouldn't be changing the subject
          would you?

                    FRANK
          Yes.

                    NATALIE
          What now?

                    FRANK
          He said, "Frank, I don't think Jason
          really understands girls."

                    NATALIE
             (laughing)
          He didn't!

                    FRANK
          He did ... "understands girls!"

                    NATALIE
          What did you say?

                    FRANK
          I said, "Give him time, Duncan."

They both break up.

                    FRANK
          I didn't know what to say! If this is how
          he is now - boy are *we* in trouble-

He stops short. The word - <u>We</u> - hangs in the air. They watch each
other, unsure of how to react. Changing the subject quickly. Frank
reaches down to the grass and comes up with one of Duncan's toys. A
real musclebound superhero. Somewhat grotesque.

                    FRANK
             (reading the tag)
          ACTION MAN?

                    NATALIE
          Richard gave it to Dunk for his birthday.

Frank sets it down.

The HEADLIGHTS OF AN APPROACHING CAR rake across ACTION MAN.

INT. ROCKLAND HIGH SCHOOL - AUDITORIUM - NIGHT

The auditorium is the only room open for summer recess. Half
a dozen girls age 12 to 18, are gathered on stage. The girls
are in shorts and T-shirts, one with a picture of Emerson and
another with the faded image of a vacation spot once visited.
Swim-suit straps are visible around some of their necks:
Earlier today they were swimming. Some look sleepy enough to
be in bed already. Ruth stands with her arms up - keeping
time and controlling the dynamics. A single girl sings "The
Drone", a low monotone one hears underneath the other voices.
They sing the Balkan folk song "Oj Savice."

                    CHORUS (SUBTITLED)
          Oh, Sava, carry me across your quiet cool
          water. There is my dear village, and in
          that village, the prettiest girl.

They shriek, they drone, they whistle. The music transports
these girls - who are normally preoccupied with images of MTV
and Brad Pitt, to a place of pure self. One of the girls -
ANNA - has a pretty serious shiner surrounding her eye. The
song ends.

                    RUTH
          That was really good! OK it's 7:30
          we should stop.

The girls gather up their things quickly.

                    RUTH
          Remember when you sing these words-
          The way we feel about the harbor, is how
          the Balkans felt about the river Sava.

The girls start out of the hall with Anna bringing up the rear.

                    RUTH
          Listen to your tapes "Moilih Ta" is still
          very rough and we've got a 40 minute
          program to get ready by Labor Day. Oh and
          Anna?

                    ANNA
          Yes Mrs. Fowler?

                    RUTH
          Next time duck!

INT. FOWLER HOUSE - NIGHT - LIVINGROOM

Ruth enters. She's beat. She starts to put her purse down when she notices:

MATT, kneeling in front of the reclining chair. It's back is to her.

                    MATT
          Just hold still ...

Ruth drops her purse and quickly comes around the recliner. Something stops her.

                    RUTH
          Oh my God.

Matt holds Frank's jaw. He gently turns his face toward the lamp.

Frank has stitches over his right eye. The blood under the white of the pupil oozing. Both lips are bright and swollen.

                    FRANK
          Dad -

                    MATT
          Come on, Frank. Hold still.

Ruth hovers, in shock.

                    RUTH
          This was her husband, wasn't it?

Frank nods wearily.

                    FRANK
          Ex, he dropped in.

He takes the compress from Matt and gingerly applies it to his forehead.

                    MATT
          Press charges.

                    FRANK
          No.

                    RUTH
          What's to stop him from doing it again?

                    MATT
          Did you hit him at all? Tell me you hit
          him! Enough so he won't want to next time?

                    FRANK
          I don't think I touched him.

Matt pulls up the skin around the bloody eye.

                         FRANK
                    Ow! Jesus, Dad!

Ruth stares at the Hospital band around Frank's wrist.

                         MATT
                    So what are you going to do?

                         FRANK
                         (smiling)
                    Take karate.

                         RUTH
                    That's not the problem.

                         FRANK
                    You know you like her.

                         RUTH
                    I like a lot of people. What about the
                    boys? Did they see it?

                         FRANK
                    They were asleep.

                         RUTH
                    Did you leave her alone with him?

                         FRANK
                    He left first. She was yelling at him. I
                    believe she had a skillet in her hand.

                         RUTH
                    Oh, for God's sake.
                         (to Matt)
                    Did you call the police?

                         MATT
                    Not yet.

                         RUTH
                    You didn't call them?

                         MATT
                    When was I going to call the police, Ruth?
                    He just got in.

Ruth scans the room.

                         RUTH
                    Where's the phone?

                         FRANK
                    MOM! hold on a second.
                    Calm down. Let's just talk about this.

Ruth wavers.

                    FRANK
          Now the cops'll go to her place first --
          and it'll scare the hell out of the kids.

                    RUTH
          Matt.

                    MATT
          We have to call them Frank.

                    FRANK
          It wasn't that serious.

                    RUTH
          Of course. Just like the relationship
          isn't serious.

                    MATT
          Ruth, this is not the time.

                    RUTH
          Well, when is the time? After he knocks
          him into a coma? This is stopping. Now.

                    FRANK
          Oh really?

                    RUTH
          Come fall, you're on a plane. Are you
          taking them with you? How do you think the
          boys will feel when you disappear?

                    FRANK
          Hey ...

                    RUTH
          This isn't just some sweetie from Vassar,
          that you'll see on holidays, Frank.
          You're not in this alone.

Frank rises and leaves the room.

                    RUTH
          Please listen. The sooner you end this
          thing the better.

Ruth exhales.

She returns to Matt, who is leaning against the recliner, chin
in hand, deep in thought.

                    RUTH
          What are we going to do?

Matt deliberates.

                    MATT
          I don't know.

                         RUTH
              ...you've got to talk to him.

                         MATT
              I don't know...I think he's right about
              scaring the kids. Why don't we call it a
              night? We'll deal with it tomorrow.

                         RUTH
              Matt are you going to call the police or
              do I have to?

                         MATT
              You just asked me what I think. If you
              want to call them, call them.

Ruth looks at him, stupefied.

Without warning, Ruth leaves and goes upstairs.

INT. FOWLER HOUSE - BEDROOM - NIGHT

Ruth lies on her side reading. Matt comes in from the
hallway, moves to the dresser and starts emptying his
pockets.

                         RUTH
              It's not the first time she's played
              around.

Matt seems relieved that she's talking to him. He sits on the
bed and starts taking off his shoes.

                         MATT
              She's not with the guy anymore.

                         RUTH
              I mean from before.

                         MATT
              What are you talking about?

                         RUTH
              Oh, come on - you've heard the same
              things I have.

                         MATT
              I think you forget. I don't take my lunch
              in the teachers' lounge -

                         RUTH
              Maybe he still loves her.

Matt looks from Ruth, out the bedroom door, and into the
hallway. He sees Frank rounding the top of the stairs.

He gets up and closes the bedroom door.

INT. FOWLER HOUSE - FRANK'S ROOM - SAME

Frank enters the room, pulls off his T-shirt and drops it on
the floor. He walks over and faces a wall mirror. He seems
nonplussed by what he sees.

INT. HENRY'S FISH SHACK - DAY

Henry Ozar sits holding court with Jason & Frank, whose facial
bruises have all but healed, the stitches replaced by a
butterfly bandage. They eat cod tongues and cheeks. Drink soda
pop from bottles.

                    HENRY
          Best part of the cod - but most
          outsiders, they won't touch it.

The shack is too warm and smells of cordage and paint,
spilled beer and male sweat. Jason is in heaven.

                    HENRY
          The summer fishermen, the part-timers,
          like Frank here - get in your hair.

                    HENRY
          There's as many as 80 of em with licenses
          now - should put up a sign - "Fish your
          own backyard or lose your traps."

Frank smiles at Jason.

                    FRANK
          A lobster is simple enough Jason. But if
          the guy going after him is even simpler -
          well he might as well give up.

                    HENRY
          Don't hurt my feelings any. Easy to talk -
          Try fishing in the winter, cold as hell
          10, 12, 20 below - no matter - Go, go,
          go, you've gotta go. You want your bread
          & flour, you gotta go.

                    FRANK
          Henry's just sore cause I catch twice as
          much as he does, with an old second hand
          Boudreau.

                    HENRY
          Don't you listen to him son - that boat
          is fine. She was my first.

Takes a sip of pop.

                    HENRY
          Kinda miss her sometimes, and that truck
          you're driving ...when you headed back to
          school, Frank?

For some reason this strikes both of them as funny and they crack up. Not Jason, he seems concerned by the question. Frank sees this.

EXT. GANGWAY - DAY

Jason heads off down the pier on his bicycle. He passes Matt.

                    JASON
          Hi, Dr. Fowler

Matt waves.

EXT. "GIGI" - SAME

Frank is hosing down the hull as Matt makes his way down the gangway.

                    MATT
          What'd you pull?

Frank glances up, then continues with his work.

                    FRANK
          Not too bad, about forty pounds.

                    MATT
          Haven't caught sight of you in days.

                    FRANK
          You know where to find me.

                    MATT
          When you coming home?

Frank turns off the spigot.

                    FRANK
          Has it come to this?

He jumps back into the boat and retrieves the bait bucket.

                    MATT
          Come to what?

Frank hops back onto the dock and sets down the container.

                    FRANK
              (smiles)
          You having to run errands for Mom.

Matt ignores the jibe. Frank starts stacking holding crates.

                    FRANK
          I'm thinking of building a couple hundred
          more traps - see if I can do better than
          break even.

Matt doesn't comment. He picks up a crate and throws it up top.

                         MATT
          It'll take you two years to get a license
          to fish off-season.

                         FRANK
          Right...unless Henry takes me on as his
          sternman.

They continue stacking.

                         MATT
          You think he'd do that?

                         FRANK
          Maybe...it's as good a life as any. Good
          enough for your father - sometimes things
          skip a generation.

                         MATT
               (trying to stay calm)
          C'mon Frank - you know you need something
          more.

                         FRANK
          Why? So I can have an Ivy League
          education like you? Christ, if it's so
          great - how come you sneak out of that
          office everyday to come down here?

                         MATT
          I like spending time with my son.

                         FRANK
               (dubious)
          uh huh.

A moment.

Frank lugs up the last container and takes a seat on the
stack. He's worn out - takes a breather.

Frank shakes his head.

                         FRANK
               (painful)
          I don't know dad...I don't know.

Matt takes a seat next to him.

A moment.

                         FRANK
          She's a wonderful girl...I see that.

Frank looks lost.

The silence is broken by a loud voice.

                         HENRY O.S.
          Frank, how long you gonna be parked
          there? I'd like to unload.

The two of them regard each other.

                         FRANK
                      (to Matt)
          Give me a hand?

                         MATT
                      (smiles)
          Sure.

INT. FOWLER HOUSE - NIGHT - STAIRWAY

Ruth comes down the stairs, wrapping her bathrobe around her.
The Dining room light is on.

THE DININGROOM

Frank sits at the table. His drafting tools are out. He's fully
immersed in a sketch.

Ruth enters quietly.

                         RUTH
          Your father is snoring. Don't mind me.

She takes a container from the fridge, smells it, makes a
quenstioning face, then puts it back - grabs another container
and opens a cupboard. Pulls out a loaf of bread.

She quietly places a sandwich in front of him, and takes a
seat.

                         RUTH
          Eat...you must be hungry.

Frank doesn't look up. his tone is flat, removed.

                         FRANK
          I'm not hungry.

                         RUTH
          Coffee?

He doesn't answer. Ruth sits there, awkwardly.

                         RUTH
          So...you talked with her?

                         FRANK
          Yep.

                         RUTH
          And...how is she?

                    FRANK
                  (sharply)
            Oh, she's great.

      I just wanted to tell you that we -
      I - liked her. Do like her. She's a
      wonderful girl...

Frank finally puts down his pencil, and looks at her.

                    FRANK
            You're not really going to have this
            conversation with me now, Ma? Are you?

Frank returns to his work. He doesn't look up again.

She leaves the food for him. Like a zoo keeper.

EXT. HARBOR - DAY

Frank hauls traps. He appears lethargic, dull - the hands a
little slower. The eyes tired. The joy of the work, replaced by
dread.

INT. HENRY'S FISH SHACK - DAY

Henry sits alone at the wooden table. There are three plates of cod,
and 3 soda-pops. Frank comes in exhausted. Henry looks up.

                    HENRY
            You're runn'in late.

Frank nods. Takes a seat, and starts in on the cod.

Henry looks at the empty seat next to Frank.

                    HENRY
            Where's our boy?

Frank ignores the question.

INT. FRANK'S TRUCK - DAY

Frank drives. Traps stacked in the bed.

He slows down to gaze out his window, as he passes

NATALIE'S HOUSE.

The truck crawls to a stop.

He takes the moment, storing each detail: Folded up lounge
chairs. Scattered toys on the porch. A tipped-over tricyle.

He idles, as if waiting for someone. After one last look he
drives off.

INT. GRINNEL HOUSE - BASEMENT - NIGHT

The sights and sounds of men gathered around a poker table. A
regular game. Everyone well into their umpteenth beer, with
the exception of Matt, who nurses a can of Moxie.

Matt frowns at his hand. He glances over to

Frank, also at the table. Frank stares at his cards, but his
mind is elsewhere.

                    WILLIS
          You can't hypnotize the cards into
          changing, Matt.

CARL, late 50's, peers above his reading glasses. He is a
lobster man by trade but fancies himself a poet.

                    WILLIS
          For Christ's sake bet - or you know
          Carl's gonna start.

Carl is indeed.

                    CARL
          "The beggar's dog and widow's cat, Feed
          them and thou wilt grow fat. The gnat that
          sings his summer's song-

Collective groans.

                    CARL
          Poison gets from slander's tongue. The
          poison of the snake and newt- Is the sweat
          of envy's foot. The poison of the honey
          bee. Is the artist's jealousy-"

                    MATT
          Alright, Carl. Two bucks.

Matt throws his two bucks in.

                    MATT
          Carl, you've really got to get off this
          Blake thing...you're in a rut.

Frank tries to smile.

                    HENRY
          Don't get him going Matt.

                    CARL
          When I do my own stuff, you guys bitch & moan.

          WILLIS   MATT
That's not true.   No! we like your stuff.

The place breaks up with laughter.

                    WILLIS
          Everybody in? Frankie you in?

Frank calls.

Hands are shown. All eyes to Frank.

                    FRANK
              (forced enthusiasm)
          Guess I'm the winner.

More groans, as Frank pulls in his winnings.

                    WILLIS
          Always the quiet ones.

The game continues ...

INT. FOWLER HOUSE - HALLWAY- DAY

Frank walks down the hallway talking on a cordless phone. His
tone casual but serious. He jots down notes in a sketch book.

                    FRANK
          Sure. Right ... I get in on the sixth. Oh,
          I'll send that out tomorrow, sir, no
          problem...Well, compared to your models -
          no, they don't compare to your models.
              (laughing)

He enters the:

BEDROOM

and plops down at his drafting table.

                    FRANK
          I'm getting another call. Can you hang on
          a second? Thanks.

Frank clicks on the other call.

                    FRANK
          Jace? Jace is that you? What's going on?

He listens.

                    FRANK
          I'll be right over.
              (firmly)
          Just stay put.

INT. NATALIE'S HOUSE - DAY

The house looks like a storm hit it: chairs tipped over, toys
scattered, papers strewn across the floor.

LIVING ROOM

Frank looks around the room. Natalie, her hair a tangled mess, her face streaked from tears, paces nervously.

She looks up at Frank.

He looks ready to explode.

                    NATALIE
          He..*just* pushed me - he didn't hit me.

                    FRANK
          Oh, he didn't hit you? Should we throw a
          party for him.

                    NATALIE
          Frank.

                    FRANK
          Enough of this. We have to call the
          police.

                    NATALIE
          I'm alright, Frank. I don't know what to
          do, okay? I hate this. I hate the kids
          seeing this.

Frank embraces her. She buries her head in his neck.

                    FRANK
          It's okay, now. Listen to me, I'm not
          going anywhere ...

INT. JASON'S BEDROOM - UPSTAIRS

Jason looks down from the window. He sees Richard's Suburban pull up front.

                    JASON O.S.
          Mom!!!

DOWNSTAIRS

A POUNDING AT THE FRONT DOOR

Natalie gives a horrified look to Frank.

                    FRANK
          Get them back upstairs.

                    NATALIE
          But...

                    FRANK
          Now.

                    NATALIE
          Come on, you guys.

Natalie hustles the boys upstairs.

THE POUNDING CONTINUES.

Frank moves to the FRONT DOOR.

He's about to check the doorknob when

THE DOORKNOB JIGGLES from the other side. It's locked.

> FRANK
> Richard, just get away from here.

Silence.

Frank turns, his eyes lock on

THE BACK-DOOR

Frank races across the living room, just as THE DOOR FLIES OPEN.

RICHARD, eyes burning, marches in.

INT. JASON'S BEDROOM - UPSTAIRS - SAME

The boys huddle around Natalie.

DUNCAN is wailing-

JASON looks terrified-

NATALIE strains to hear-

SOMETHING CRASHES FROM DOWNSTAIRS-

WE HEAR RICHARD AND FRANK YELLING.

NATALIE starts to the door-

> NATALIE
> Listen kids - Stay here.

DUNCAN won't let go of her sleeve. He starts to move with her.

> NATALIE
> (screaming)
> I said stay here!

He lets go and,

JASON takes him up in his small arms.

> JASON
> (to Duncan)
> It's OK Dunk...Mommy's coming
> back.

NATALIE hesitates - then heads out the door.

We MOVE WITH HER out the bedroom to the:

TOP OF THE STAIRS.

She slowly steps down the stairs.

A GUNSHOT.

SHE SCREAMS.

>   NATALIE
>   FRANK!

She moves quickly down the stairs.

Cautiously - she looks over the landing.

HER P.O.V.: From above, Richard stands, his back to her, his head hung.

In his hand. a 9mm Pistol.

Natalie lets out a plaintive wail.

>   NATALIE
>   NO...

Emotionless, Richard turns to her - looks down at the floor -
then starts toward the kitchen.

Natalie races down the steps and stops.

FRANKS'S BODY ON THE FLOOR. HIS FACE IS HALF BLOWN AWAY.

She's paralyzed, a scream trapped somewhere inside.

She turns away.

>   JASON O.S.   DUNCAN O.S.
>   (screaming)   (crying)
>   MOMMY! DUNCAN'S COMING   LET GO OF ME!!!
>   DOWNSTAIRS!

Richard sits at the kitchen table.

The gun rests in front of him.

His right sleeve is splattered with Frank's blood.

BLACK

FADE IN:

THE SCREEN FILLS WITH AN OPAQUE DARK SURFACE. A LIGHT APPEARS.

INT. UNION CLINIC - LAB ROOM - DAY

Matt's face appears distorted behind the surface.

                    JANELLE O.S.
                (frightened)
            Matt?

He lowers what we now see to be an X-Ray and kills the light.

MATT'S OFFICE

He hesitates, presses the blinking hold button, picks up the receiver.

                    MATT
            Hello?...Hello? Natalie?

The blood drains from his face.

WE HEAR THE DISTANT SOUNDS OF MACEDONIA.

INT. ROCKLAND HIGH SCHOOL - HALL - DUSK

Matt stands in the hallway outside of the auditorium that is Ruth's classroom. A banner across the hall reads HAVE A WONDERFUL SUMMER, SEE YOU IN THE FALL.

The choir finishes the last strains. Ruth is happy the rehearsal has gone well. She smiles in a way that expresses the simple joy she will never know again.

                    RUTH
            Great.

The girls gather their things and start out, laughing and running after each other. Matt stands in the hallway as they rush past.

BLACK

FADE IN:

EXT. ST. FRANCIS CEMETERY - DAY

Frank's casket is lowered into the ground.

A large gathering of relatives and friends stand before Father Oberti as he finishes the eulogy.

Matt's arm is tightly interlocked with Ruth's, beneath her eyes - swelling from three days of suffering. Their hands clenched together make one fist, both parents keeping the other upright.

Matt steps up to Frank's open grave.

The gathering watches as Matt peers down into the hole, silently speaking to it. He reaches down, grabs a fistful of dirt. Then tosses it into the open grave.

Matt pauses, staring down, into the hole ...

He steps back, as Father Oberti delivers the end of his eulogy.

Matt looks blankly around, noticing the family's many friends, including; Carl and Henry from the game, Willis and Katie, and Frank's friend, Tim.

Matt's eyes linger on someone behind Tim:

A LONE FEMALE FIGURE IN BLACK, away from the crowd. Natalie.

Their eyes meet.

Matt, almost imperceptibly, nods.

INT. FOWLER HOUSE - DAY

A large casserole is placed on a long table with many assorted dishes. A HAND REACHES IN, scoops up some of the casserole onto a small plate, and carries it to

A SMALL CLUSTER OF PEOPLE

standing in the middle of a much larger gathering, the reception after the funeral.

Matt stands in the downstairs hallway. He looks around the room, as if it is all a dream.

Children getting soda pop. Others in conversation. The odd person looks up at him, then turns away.

Willis steps up to Matt.

His wife, Katie, stands nearby.

Matt doesn't seem to notice Willis.

Willis puts a gentle hand on his friend's arm.

                    WILLIS
                 (softly)
          Can I get you anything?

Matt suddenly looks up at them, as if confused.

                    MATT
          Where's Ruth?

KATIE
She went to lie down, Matt.

He turns and heads upstairs. Willis and Katie watch him go.

UPSTAIRS HALL

Matt approaches their bedroom. The door is ajar.

BEDROOM

He steps in, to Ruth, who is on the bed. Her back is to him, apparently sleeping. Crumbled tissues litter the bed, the floor.

Matt quietly moves to her. He reaches down, about to touch her head. Something stops him.

He turns, and leaves.

UPSTAIRS HALL

Frank's room is facing him. Instinctively, he goes to open the door, then pauses.

FRANK'S ROOM

Matt slowly enters. He looks around, as if freezing the room in his memory.

The place is untouched. Frank's many sketches are still pinned to the wall. Some clothes lie scattered on the floor. His fishing cap.

Matt starts to pick up. He takes Frank's clothes from the floor and places them on his bed.

He looks at a dirty T-shirt in his hand. He brings it to his face. He inhales deeply, able to smell his son's lingering scent-

Finally, he sets the shirt on the bed. Wanders around. Strays near Frank's drafting table-

He reaches out, touching the table, grazing the topography of scattered pencils - drawings strewn across it- The Froebel Gifts.

He takes a seat at the table. Feeling its frame, the sketches, the seat below-

And without warning he is overcome. He lurches forward, burying his face in his hands. The sobs come unrestrained, violently, like a sudden tidal wave.

BLACK

FADE IN:

INT. FOWLER HOUSE - DEN - NIGHT - 2 WEEKS LATER

A LAUGH-TRACK fills the air.

Ruth in pajamas and bathrobe, watches a stand-up comic on TV.
She sips tea from a mug.

Matt appears at the door, kettle in hand.

                         MATT
            Some more?

Ruth looks up and nods.

BLACK

FADE IN:

EXT. FOWLER HOUSE - DAY

THE FRONT LAWN

Matt stands atop a ladder underneath a large Maple, he
struggles with a pair of pruning shears. At war with a large
branch - the branch seems to be winning.

INT. FOWLER HOUSE - UPSTAIRS HALL - SAME

Ruth, still dressed in her robe, pads down the hallway.
Stops to glance out the window at

MATT - working.

EXT. FOWLER HOUSE - SAME

Ruth stands transfixed. REFLECTED IN THE WINDOW PANE BELOW
HER FACE: WE SEE

Quick glimpses through branches, of a small boy scampering up a
tree. Flashes of arms, legs, a smile.

We can make out the GIGGLES of the child, but they are
distorted, wobbly, as if deteriorated by memory.

The tree shudders as the boy climbs higher.

            MATT O.S.   RUTH O.S.
Okay - watch it now, Frank.   Frank, listen to your father.
That's high enough ...

The tree continues shaking.

Ruth allows the memory, then turns back and pads back down the
hallway.

BLACK

FADE IN:

INT. UNION CLINIC - MATT'S OFFICE - DAY

Matt sits behind his desk catching up on some paperwork.
Janelle appears in the doorway.

                    JANELLE
          I'm going to lunch Dr. Fowler--

                    MATT
          ...alright

She continues smiling, as though trying to extend her tenderness. Matt
avoids eye contact. She Leaves. Matt looks relieved.

INT. GRINNEL'S CROW'S NEST - DAY

Willis opened this place after serving as a chief petty officer
in the Vietnam War. The theme, if there is one, is definitely
nautical. Snapshots of longtime customers are stapled on the
walls between the booths and tables, two are framed, and
prominent. They are from Willis's Navy days; The first, an
entry photo of A YOUNG WILLIS smiling in front of the flag. The
second a sun faded color photo of Matt and Willis. Both look
to be in their twenties, both dressed in navy whites.

The trade here is mostly very early breakfast, and then lunch
for the men who work at the leather and shoe factories.

A MUTED news show plays on a ceiling TV at the far end of the
booths. A sign on the wall reads _Try our "Forget about lunch"_
breakfast.

Willis carries over two plates with omelettes, parks them on
the table, and takes a seat across from Matt.

                    WILLIS
          Don't worry, I didn't make em.

Matt takes a bite. He winces.

                    WILLIS
          What? Oh, that's mine.

He switches plates.

                    WILLIS
          Sorry.

Matt takes another bite. Better.

                    WILLIS
          You got back to work so quick, Matt. It's
          not too soon?

                    MATT
          I can't stay home. So, how's business?

                    WILLIS
          Oh, you know, same old crap. Got held up
          again, you knew that.

                    MATT
          No. I didn't.

                    WILLIS
          yeah...they got seventy-five bucks.

                    MATT
          Were you on the till?

Willis chuckles, shakes his head.

                    WILLIS
          They would have gotten something else if
          I'd been on the till.

Matt nods.

                    WILLIS
          How you doin', Matt?
          You don't write, you don't call. Where'd
          the love go?

                    MATT
          Nag nag nag.

Matt glances at an old clipping from the BOSTON GLOBE stapled
to the wall. It's a photo from the 67 Redsox dream team.
Petrocelli, Yaztremski and Reggie Smith, each hold up two
fingers, they are smiling after hitting consecutive homeruns.
Matt remembers. Happier days.

                    WILLIS
          They set the bail hearing yet?

                    MATT
          Sometime in the next few days.yeah,

                    WILLIS
          Are you going?

                    MATT
          I don't know. Davis says it's a formality
          really. I haven't talked to Ruth about
          whether she thinks we should go or not.

                    WILLIS
          If it's too much for Ruth, I'll come with
          you Matt.

                    MATT
          Thanks, but I'm sure it'll be alright--
          Davis says it's a formality really.

                    WILLIS
          The criminal trial set yet?

                    MATT
          October.

                    WILLIS
          October?

                    MATT
          That's what they tell me, anyway.

                    WILLIS
          Christ, they take their time.

                    MATT
          ...yeah, well, he's in there now.

                    WILLIS
          They're keeping him busy, I'm sure - You
          know where they'll move him once he's
          sentenced?

Matt shifts the focus to his omelette.

                    MATT
          You have any Tabasco sauce?

Willis pauses. He looks around, calls out to the kitchen.

                    WILLIS
          Hey, Pete. Tabasco. Pete! Ah, shit.

He heads to the back. Matt looks out the window. A refrigerated
truck with the STROUT logo on its side pulls to a stop at the
light. Willis returns with sauce in hand.

He takes a seat. Shifts his tone again.

                    WILLIS
          Next weekend Matt. We really want you to
          come up to the camp. Katie's insisting.
          Not to pressure you or anything. But if
          you don't come she's going to invite her
          sister and that idiot, and I know I'm
          going to wind up insulting him again.

Matt considers this.

                    WILLIS
          The future of my family is in your hands.

                    MATT
          Let me ask Ruth.

                    WILLIS
          You know, your seat is getting cold at the
          game. We have Carl's kid subbing for you.
          Not that we mind - he loses every time.
          But we'd rather take your money.

                    MATT
              (smiling)
          Thanks.

Matt stares aimlessly out the window.

Willis goes back to his eggs.

Both men comfortable enough with each other to be silent.

                    WILLIS
          How's Ruth doing?

                    MATT
          Alright. Her...her car broke down.

                    WILLIS
          Always something.

THE PHONE RINGS OVER:

INT. FOWLER HOUSE - LIVING ROOM - DAY

The phone continues to ring. Then stops. Ruth lies on the
couch, dressed in her robe. Her hair looks neglected. She
stares at the television. An ad for Sudbay Chevrolet comes on
the screen - a testimonial from a bald man saying "The best
thing about the sales people is they're not pushy." A large
graphic plays over the man's face NOT PUSHY. WE HEAR a car
pull into the driveway. Ruth doesn't seem to notice. An ad
for a long-term residential nursing retirement center. Ruth
looks interested.

The front door opens and Matt comes in with groceries.

                    RUTH
               (not looking up)
          How was your day?

Matt carries the bags into the kitchen.

                    MATT O.S.
          Fine. Saw Willis--

                    RUTH
          My day was fine, too, thanks.

Matt comes out of the kitchen.

                    MATT
          Sorry...how was your day?
          Tried calling - thought you might have
          gone out. The Grinnel's invited us up to
          the camp next weekend. Said I'd check with
          you, if we had other plans ...

                    RUTH
          That sounds fine.

He turns, a little surprised.

                    MATT
          We don't have to.

She looks up at him.

                    RUTH
          You don't want to go?

                    MATT
               (weakly)
          No, I want to ...

                    RUTH
          Great. Tell them yes.

                    MATT
               (hopeful)
          I thought you might be busy getting the
          girls ready.

No answer. She's back into her show.

THE KITCHEN

The sink still has the plates and cups from breakfast. Matt starts
to clean up. Reaching for a dishrag on the counter, he notices the
blinking of the answering machine. There are a half dozen messages.
He hits play. Nothing. He finds the volume.

                    V.O.
          Hello, Mr. & Mrs. Fowler, this is Regina
          at the District attorney's office -
          Mr.Davis would like to speak with you
          both just as soon as possible.

INT. KNOX COUTY COURTHOUSE - DAY

A windowless rotunda. JUDGE WILLIAM WILKENSON presides.

CLOSE WILKENSON

                    WILKENSON
          Mr. Strout has been in the custody of the
          Knox County Sherrif's Department since
          August second, held without bail.The
          court is obliged to hold a bail hearing
          within two weeks of incarceration, which
          is the purpose of our procedings here
          today. Given the schedule considerations
          on this docket, the court feels that we
          should conduct the probable cause hearing
          in tandem. Witnesses will be called at
          this time. Unless there are any
          objections to the contrary this court
          will recess until 2:00 p.m.

EXT. KNOX COUNTY COURTHOUSE - DAY

Natalie comes up the brick walk and enters the building.

INT. KNOX COUNTY COURTHOUSE - LATER

A gray concrete room, washed out by the buzzing overhead florescent.

Matt and Ruth sit on metal fold-out chairs, alongside twenty or so spectators, and a smattering of reporters, in the gallery.

Richard, unkempt and dressed in an ORANGE JUMPSUIT, sits patiently next to one of his two attorneys.

Matt and Ruth glance over at

NATHAN STROUT, 62, sitting directly behind Richard.

Nathan's two other sons, both big men like Richard, sit at his side.

Nathan feels the Fowlers' stares. His eyes stay focused on the front of the room.

Richard's trial attorney, MARLA KEYES, 30's, smart, expensive, and a long way from her home in Boston, stands in the COURT WELL.

Natalie Strout in the witness box.

                    MARLA KEYES
          So, Mr. Fowler had asked you to go
          upstairs with your children as your
          husband was trying to enter...

DISTRICT ATTORNEY WILLIAM DAVIS, 40, rises.

                    DAVIS
          Objection. Mrs. Strout's police interview
          is already documented, the defense has a
          copy of it. There's no reason to waste
          anymore of the court's time ...

                    MARLA KEYES
          Your Honor, we just want to review exactly
          what Mrs. Strout saw on the afternoon of
          July 17th. Isn't that why we're here?

The judge nods.

                    JUDGE
          Overruled.
               (to Natalie)
          Please continue.

Natalie tries to recapture her place. Keyes nods.

                    MARLA KEYES
               (recapping)
          So you were bringing your children up to
          their bedroom ...

Natalie's glance wanders to the gallery, to Matt and Ruth.

She sits on her hands to keep them from shaking.

                    NATALIE
          ...Right. I was in Jason and Dunk's room - I
          didn't know what was happening downstairs. I was
          getting worried. I asked Jason to read Dunk a
          story. He didn't want a story - He wanted to come
          with me...so I sat him back down on the bunk -
          and I left them in the room.

                    MARLA KEYES
          You left "them"?

                    NATALIE
          My *boys*.

She starts to cry.

                    MARLA KEYES
               (softly)
          Of course. I'm sorry. Go on.

                    NATALIE
          I closed the door...I moved down the hall. I
          looked back to make sure they weren't behind me.
          I had just started down the stairs, when I heard
          the shot.   I ran down...

A deep sob ...

                    NATALIE
          ...and Richard...

                    MARLA KEYES
          I'm sorry, can we just back up? You said
          you "heard the shot"?

                    NATALIE
          Yes.

                    MARLA KEYES
          You "*heard*"? Mrs. Strout, did you witness
          the accident?

Prosecutor Davis jumps up.

                    DAVIS
          Objection. There are no grounds to
          indicate this was an "*accident*."

The judge nods.

                    JUDGE
               (to stenographer)
          Please strike "accident" from the record.
               (to Marla Keyes)
          Ms. Keyes, please rephrase the question.

Marla Keyes hasn't taken her eyes off Natalie. They both know
what's next.

                              MARLA KEYES
                         (gently)
                    Mrs. Strout...did you actually witness
                    the firearm discharge?

INT. DISTRICT ATTORNEY'S OFFICE - DAY

Davis hands a cup of coffee to Matt, who sits on a faux leather
couch with Ruth.

                              DAVIS
                         (to Ruth re: coffee)
                    You sure you don't want?

                              RUTH
                    I'm fine.

Davis takes a seat across from them.

                              DAVIS
                    You see, we can't appeal bail. It's just
                    not set up that way.

                              RUTH
                    You let that bastard walk out and we're
                    supposed to just sit here? Don't tell us
                    there's nothing to do about this.

                              DAVIS
                    It's not us, Mrs. Fowler. The state's bail
                    code is to ensure future court appearances -

                              DAVIS
                    In this case Strout's family was prepared to
                    put up a substantial amount of property as
                    bail - That, along with his ties to the
                    community made it hard for us to convince the
                    judge of a serious "Risk of Flight".

                              RUTH
                    Oh - I see.

                              DAVIS
                    It's not just your case. Now you can file a civil
                    suit. I recommend it. But not now, wait till
                    after the crimminal trial.

Matt stares at a small cartoonish statue on Davis's desk. It is
one of those things that were popular in the 70's. A little man
chasing an ambulance. It reads "World's Greatest Lawyer."

                              RUTH
                    And when will that be? Next week, next
                    month?

                              DAVIS
                    Well...honestly - anywhere between twelve
                    and eighteen months?

> RUTH
> I thought you said there would be a jury
> trial sometime in October!?

> DAVIS
> If he was incarcerated the judge would
> move for an October date - basically to
> save the County the cost of housing and
> feeding him as an inmate - But with bail
> the court date, unfortunately, is always
> later.

> RUTH
> Oh my God, oh my God.

Matt jumps in.

> MATT
> But you're confident you'll be able to put
> him away for good then... Right?

Davis looks uncomfortable with the question.

Ruth sees this. She gathers herself.

> RUTH
> The things she said in there...what is the
> damage?

> DAVIS
> Manslaughter.

> RUTH
> What? Oh, Jesus Christ!

> DAVIS
> The way this is going, that'd
> be my bet - especially since
> Nathan Strout brought up that
> barracuda from Boston - she's
> very smart.

> RUTH
> This was no accident. He killed our son in
> cold blood.

> MATT
> Ruth.

> RUTH
> What?

> MATT
> How long would he be sent away for?

> DAVIS
> Hard to say really. Anywhere between five
> to fifteen years. We think we have a good
> shot at the max - fifteen. Even with good
> behavior, he'd do a full ten.

                         RUTH
          Ten years? Five years? Are you out of your
          mind!? He killed my son. Does anyone know
          this?

Matt looks at his shoes, as Ruth glares down Davis.

Davis sits back, a little shook up.

                         DAVIS
          I'm sorry, Mrs. Fowler. I understand.
          Unfortunately, in situations like this
          when there is no eye witness, there ...
          well, there's not a lot we can do.

INT. MATT'S CAR - DAY - MOVING

Matt drives. Ruth looks out the windshield.

Both in their own worlds.

Ruth turns to look out her side window.

THE CANNERY'S STACKS ARE HUMPING.

THE CAR DRIVES PAST THE SITE.

EXT. FOWLER HOUSE - DAY

A handful of reporters and photographers lingering on the
lawn, are galvanized by the arrival of the Fowlers.

INT. FOWLER HOUSE - DAY

Ruth is just entering, jostled, relieved to be home.

She turns. Matt's not there. She looks out the front door to
see

MATT AT THE BASE OF THE LAWN

surrounded by reporters.

                              REPORTER #1
               Dr. Fowler, how do you feel about Richard
               Strout's bail?

                              REPORTER #2
               Do you plan to take any further legal
               action, Dr. Fowler?

                              REPORTER #3
               Dr. Fowler, have you had any contact with
               Mr. Strout?

Matt stands paralyzed, a deer caught in the headlights.

THE KITCHEN

Matt enters as Ruth takes the plates to the sink. She keeps her back to him. He pulls off his coat.

>   MATT
>   Can you believe this? I ask those idiots to
>   leave. No one budges. Not one. What the hell
>   are we supposed to do, bring them sandwiches?

>   RUTH
>   (her back to him)
>   What are you asking for?

>   MATT
>   What?

Ruth turns to him.

>   RUTH
>   (sharply)
>   If you want them to leave. Tell them to
>   leave.

INT. FOWLER HOUSE - BEDROOM - NIGHT

Ruth is asleep. Matt stares at the ceiling. He turns to the clock. It's after three.

KITCHEN

He opens a cupboard door and grabs some Fig Newtons. He stands there eating them, the door of the cupboard is long, the kind you see in old capes. Matt stares at the inside of the door. His finger slides down the length, he kneels down.

We see what he's looking at. Pen and pencil marks, straight lines - each about two inches apart - each with Frank's name and age.

THE DEN

Matt sits in his chair. The TV plays, muted. He's looks at it, but he's not watching.

Finally, he rises, clicks the TV off with the remote, and flicks off the light.

EXT. RICHARD STROUT'S DUPLEX - NIGHT

A small development of modest, duplex apartment buildings. The architecture is outdated, the landscape unkempt.

CLOSER ON one corner unit. The lights are off; there is no sign of life.

A Brown Suburban sits in the driveway.

WE HEAR the RADIO "The following is a rebroadcast of last night's game, the third in a four game series at Fenway-

INT. MATT'S CAR - NIGHT

Matt, wearing a light coat over his pajamas, sits behind the
wheel of his car <u>listening to the game.</u>

He glances down at a piece of paper with an address. Then back
out his windshield, looking at the corner duplex unit.

INT. FOWLER HOUSE - KITCHEN - DAY

Ruth sits at the table in her bathrobe. Smoking. The CAMDEN
HERALD in one hand. The COURIER GAZETTE, and THE WORKING
WATERFRONT within easy reach.

Matt enters, fully dressed in jeans and a sweater. He winces at
the smoke.

                    RUTH
          You slept late. For you.

Matt pours himself some coffee.

                    MATT
          I took one of your pills.

                    RUTH
          You never do that.

She turns the page, absorbed in an article.

Shaking her head, she slaps the paper down.

                    RUTH
          Well, there it is in black and white. You
          should read some of the things he says.
          Unbelievable.

Matt takes a sip of coffee. He glances down at the paper.

He nods, without really looking.

                    MATT
          Yeah.

He checks his watch.

                    MATT
          I should get going.

                    RUTH
          Where? It's Saturday.

                    MATT
          I won't be gone long.

He bends, kisses her lightly on the cheek.

                              MATT
                    I'm meeting Willis. I'll tell him we're
                    coming.

She stares at the kitchen doorway long after he exits.

Finally, she pulls the paper back and resumes reading.

INT. CANDY'S QUICK SHOP - DAY

Natalie stands behind the only counter of a small MOM AND POP
STORE whose specialty is cold beer, wine, cigarettes, and fish
& game licenses. She rings up some items for a couple of
teenagers.

Matt enters the place, keeping his distance, a few feet from
the counter.

Natalie sees him.

She pauses, as if quickly trying to gather her thoughts, the
teenagers are waiting for their change.

She counts it back to them, and they exit.

Matt steps forward.

                              MATT
                    Hi.

                              NATALIE
                    ...Hi.

An elderly woman places a half-gallon of milk, a dozen eggs,
and a carton of L&M cigarettes down on the register counter.

Natalie quickly rings up the items and bags them.

                         ELDERLY WOMAN
                    Can you break a fifty?

Natalie takes the bill, places it in a drawer underneath the
register, and hands the woman her change, with a smile.

                         ELDERLY WOMAN
                    Thank you, dear.

                              NATALIE
                    You're welcome.

                         ELDERLY WOMAN
                    Could I possibly get another bag?

Natalie quickly double bags the woman's groceries.

There is a break in the customer flow. Natalie steps to the end
of the counter.

                         MATT
          I just wanted to see how you're doing. I
          tried reaching you ...

                         NATALIE
          Oh. We're at my mother's house now. I'm
          sorry, I wanted to call you ...

                         MATT
          It's okay.

She looks over. <u>A man hovers over some magazines near the
register.</u>

                         NATALIE
                    (almost whispering)
          Dr. Fowler...I'm so...I don't even know
          how to begin...

                         MATT
          You don't have to.

                         NATALIE
          I didn't lie the first time, I didn't,
          it's just - how it came out. I'm so sorry.

Matt nods, as if he had assumed as much.

                         NATALIE
          Is Mrs. Fowler...does she know you're
          here?

The Man places a 12-pack of beer on the counter. Natalie looks
to Matt, who shakes his head *no*.

Natalie steps back to the register and rings up the beer.

Her chin quivers. She makes a mistake on the register, has to
start over.

A few more customers gather on line.

                         NATALIE
                    (to customer)
          Can I get you anything else?

She rings him up. Makes change as another customer steps up.

Matt steps near her, trying to maintain privacy.

                         MATT
                    (quietly)
          How are the boys? Are they okay?

Natalie, choked by emotion, cannot respond. Near tears, she
puts her hand up, unable to speak.

Matt reaches out to touch her arm.

His gesture is interrupted as:

She pulls the cigarettes from an overhead rack. The Man pays.

Matt stays a moment longer. There's nothing else to say.

He leaves.

She returns to her job.

EXT. ST. FRANCIS CEMETERY - ADJACENT CHURCH - DAY

We see Ruth from a good distance away, watched from afar. She places some potted daisies on a grave. She kneels down.

EXT. ST. FRANCIS CHURCH - PARKING LOT - LATER

Ruth walks through an empty lot and heads for her car.

RUTH'S CAR

She opens the door. Suddenly there is a hand on her shoulder. She is startled.

She turns around. It's Father Oberti.

EXT. ST. FRANCIS CEMETERY - LATER

Ruth and Father Oberti sit smoking on a bench.

                    RUTH
          It comes in waves...and then nothing. Like
          a *rest* in music. No sound - but *so* loud.

A moment.

                    RUTH
          I don't know what to do.

 Father Oberti nods.

                    RUTH
          I feel so *angry*.

Father Oberti looks off in the distance.

                    FATHER OBERTI
          Louise McVey lost a child a few years
          back. Maybe you remember.

                    RUTH
                (searching)
          Mmmm she had four - it was the youngest
          girl, wasn't it?

                    FATHER OBERTI
          Yes. She told me about a vision she had
          when she found out her daughter had
          died...she saw herself at a great
          distance from the earth - and encircling
          it, an endless line - as she got closer
          she saw that it was made up of mothers -

                          FATHER OBERTI
          traveling forward.   She fell into line,
          and began walking with them.   When they
          reached a certain point, the line
          divided.   She said she knew - that all the
          millions of women on her side - were the
          mothers who had lost children...she
          seemed to find great comfort in that.

Ruth doesn't react.

                          RUTH
          How did she die?

                          FATHER OBERTI
          A drowning...some kind of swimming
          accident.

                          RUTH
          Oh.

EXT. FOWLER HOUSE - DAY

A mower moves across the lawn, spitting up a shower of grass.

Matt pushes the mower.

INT. YVONNE'S SPECIALTY SHOPPE - DAY

A small boutique frequented by mature women. Blouses with a *flair*,
pantsuits, and *nice* dresses hang from the racks. The sort of place a
woman can still buy a pair Jozefa white gloves. The front of the store
is devoted to footwear.

Ruth sits while YVONNE, 45, kneels in front of her, holding
Ruth's stockinged foot. She slips on a dress shoe.

                          YVONNE
          Oh, they're beautiful on you Ruth.

Ruth stands up, takes a few steps.

She stares at the shoes.

They are a rich black.

                          RUTH
          Do you have them in brown?

                          YVONNE
          I think so, let me check.

Yvonne disappears into the back.

Ruth walks to the front of the store, browsing.

She moves to the display window and brings a pair of very
young pumps up to her nose, and inhales. She smiles and sets
the shoes back on the ledge.

Something OUTSIDE catches her attention.

EXT. YVONNE'S SPECIALTY SHOPPE - SAME TIME -

The REFLECTION OF A COUPLE, walking down the sidewalk, can be glimpsed in the window, their movement WASHES ACROSS RUTH'S FACE.

ON THE COUPLE.

a YOUNG BLOND WOMAN holding hands with a dark haired, young man.

As he turns to smile at her. We see his face.

RICHARD.

Oblivious to Ruth's presence.

INT. YVONNE'S SPECIALTY SHOPPE - SAME TIME -

Ruth looks disoriented.

                    YVONNE O.S.
          I'm sorry Ruth - there's only the black.

She turns from the window. Yvonne stands next to her, an open shoe box in her hands.

EXT. FOWLER HOUSE - DRIVEWAY - LATER

Two Hefty bags are dragged along the walk. Matt tosses one next to a garbage that sits just inside the garage. He picks up the other bag tossing it inside.

The bottom splits and grass spills out onto the driveway. He goes inside and returns with a broom.

He sweeps the grass into a pile. Picking up handfuls and refilling the bag. He takes the broom and sweeps what's left back toward the lawn. He stops, stares down at his feet.

IN THE CEMENT; A child's handprints and writing, <u>Frank 82</u>

Ruth's car pulls into the driveway.

She gets out, almost slamming the car door.

Without a word, she moves past Matt, and into the house.

Matt continues sweeping.

INT. FOWLER HOUSE - BEDROOM - NIGHT - LATER

Ruth wakes to the sound of metal on metal. She looks over to Matt, he's not there.

                    RUTH
               (scared)
          Matt?

She steps to the window, pulls back the shears and looks out.

Through the window, in the dark, alone, flashlight in hand.

<u>Matt is dismantling the swing set.</u>

INT. GRINNEL CABIN - DAY

A four room dwelling, surrounded by a wraparound porch that
looks out over a canopy of forest below. The place was built
before insulation was practical. Planks, beams, and studs are
exposed. There is a bathroom, two bedrooms, and a common room
consisting of a kitchen/dining area, and living room, with a
large, river stone fireplace.

There are two oil burning lamps hanging from crossbeams at each
end of the room. Ruth sits next to Katie at a table in the
middle of the room. Katie is pouring over a stack of snapshot
books, desribing her children and grandchildren in each pose.
The photos, while many, are all from a single trip that the
family made to Florida. There is a clear difference in
vernacular between the two women, Katie also has a voice that
has been trained to reach anyone who might be in the far
corners of her house.

                    KATIE
          Oh and here's lil Charles down at the
          pool. He figured out how to get down to
          the pool on the elevator all by himself.

                    RUTH
               (patiently)
          He must of been very proud.

                    KATIE
          Oh yeah. Oh here's Shannon waitin in line
          for that rollercoaster - You know the
          one?

Ruth has no idea.

                    RUTH
               (Politely)
          Were the lines very long?

                    KATIE
          Well some of em...yeah - sixty minutes
          and upward. Unless of coarse ya got the
          "Fast-Pass."

                    RUTH
          What's the fast pass?

                    KATIE
          Well ya got all the different "Kingdoms"
          there...and so you take the fast pass -
          it's a kind of a laminated card and you
          put it intah a machine and it tells you
          what time to come back - so you can go
          right in without waitin in line. You guys
          ever go down to Florida?

Ruth smiles at the thought and shakes her head.

>
RUTH
...no. How many grandchildren do you
have now?

Katie turns from the snapshots and takes a breath while
holding up her fingers to count.She is genuinely unsure.

>
KATIE
(under her breath)
Well there's lil Charles, Shannon, the
three older ones and the babies...eleven.

>
RUTH
That must wonderful.

Katie smiles and nods. It is.

>
KATIE
(by rote)
Well, Willis always says "I guess there's
no danger of us dying off --

She catches herself. Too late. She looks at Ruth. Embarrassed.

>
KATIE
I'm sorry - I wasn't...

Ruth waves her off good naturedly.

>
RUTH
I wanted to have more...but we had Frank,
and Matt was just starting his practice..
...I guess it made sense.

>
KATIE
(guileless)
Well sometimes I wished I was an only
child - let me tell you. When I was
little, my big sister could get me to do
anything. More than once she got me to
throw myself down the stairs by telling
me the blanket she wrapped me in was a
magic carpet. Naturally, not being that
swift, I believed her. Plus which, on
this trip to Florida, we was in one of
the Kingdoms there, and she was going on
about how's we had to go on this one ride
that was in this sort of mountain.
I said "OK as long as it's not a roller
coaster-- on account of my back." Well,
we get strapped intah the little car
there - she starts laughing - Oh it's a
rollercoaster alright - that one there.

She points to the pictures.

>
KATIE (cont'd)
A ride in the dark, no less.

EXT. GRINNEL CABIN - SAME

A great, endless, expanse of fir trees.

We are far up, looking out at this timbered landscape that
seems to stretch forever.

Matt stands before the edge of a cliff, dressed in a short
sleeved shirt. He takes a deep breath of the crisp mountain
air.

A steady CHOPPING rhythm is heard in the background.

Matt turns. Willis is chopping the last of some firewood.

                    MATT
          How much of this is yours?

Willis plants his axe in the stump.

                    WILLIS
               (smiling)
          You ask me that every time. You know the cove, the
          other side of the cabin?

                    MATT
          yeah ...?

                    WILLIS
          All the way to the other shoreline.

Matt turns to him, grinning.

                    WILLIS
          Almost three hundred and fifty acres.
          Know what it went for when I bought it?
          You don't want to know.

Matt continues surveying, awed.

Willis turns, starts walking back to his chore.

                    WILLIS
          Come on, I'll let you help me.

Matt joins him. Together, they bundle up the wood.

TRAIL TO GRINNEL CABIN - DAY

Matt and Willis load the wood into a small trailer attached to
a GREEN POLARIS MAGNUM 500 ATV.

                    WILLIS
          Only got 1/2 a chord of oak left at home -
          and you know how much that bastard Daniels
          charges - least I can stack this up to the
          cabin...have something to burn this fall.

TRAIL TO CABIN - SAME - MOVING

Matt sits behind Willis on the ATV as they pull the wood up the
road. The trees clear and we see the cabin. A GREEN SUBARU
FORESTER is parked in front.

INT. GRINNEL CABIN - DAY

Willis, Katie, Matt and Ruth, sit around a copious holiday
spread, well into their meal.

                    KATIE
          It's a wonderful product and they treat you
          pretty good. It was on account of selling Mary
          Kay, that we got the new Subaru.

                    RUTH
               (small talk)
          The ride up was very comfortable. It's a
          very nice car.

                    WILLIS
          Well it's not really a car, it's got four-wheel drive.
          It's a little SUV.

The Grinnel's custom, is to loudly, and with very little effort,
finish each others sentences. This is how they have fun.

                    KATIE
          What the hell is that SUV crap?

                    WILLIS
          Sports utility vehicle.

                    KATIE
               (to Matt and Ruth)
          It's a little Jeep. SUV, ATV, KFC - what's
          with all these...?

She searches for the word. Little help? Anyone, anyone?

                    RUTH
               (finally)
          Acronyms.

                    KATIE
          Yeah, guess it's too much trouble to just
          say what something is anymore.

                    WILLIS
               (to the table)
          What does PMS stand for?

                    KATIE
          Yeah well, I was an army brat.
          I grew up with Jeeps. Willy is just
          uncomfortable that I know more about *one*
          masculine thing than he does.

                    MATT
          Just one?

The party chuckles.

                    WILLIS
          Thanks, buddy.

Matt helps himself to the last of the wine. He seems to have
had quite a bit.

Ruth watches as he drains the bottle.

She shoots him a look.

He catches it.

A moment.

                    RUTH
               (looking away)
          You've done a such a nice job here, Katie.
          Don't tell me you made those drapes
          yourself...is that antique linen?

                    KATIE
               (laughing)
          Sort of..

She walks over to the window and fingers the fabric.

                    KATIE
          They're pillowcases from our first house.

Ruth smiles at the memory. Katie sits back down at the table.

                    KATIE
          Oh, I've saved every knick-knack & whim-wham we
          ever had.

EXT. DIRT ROAD - DAY

A post stands proudly at the end of a dirt and gravel road.
Attached to it are two signs. One reads PRIVATE ROAD. The
other, NO HUNTING.

It butts up against two lanes of blacktop - a small logging
road.

Headlights cut through the early evening.

Willis's idea of a SUV; a green, SUBARU FORESTER, kicks up some
rocks. It pauses briefly before taking a right onto the pavement.

INT/EXT. SUBARU - TREVETT SWING BRIDGE - DAY

The car is stopped behind a wooden guard arm. A swing bridge
opens for a large fishing boat. The bridge is operated by one
man. He uses a long metal tool, that he loops into a pulley
system, which lies beneath a grid in the center of the
bridge.

EXT. TREVITT BRIDGE - SUBARU - DAY

Ruth asleep in the back seat, it's been a long weekend. Matt glances over at her, then up to the front

We are outside the car as it waits for the drawbridge to close, so it may continue. We hear the following from perspective.

                    MATT
          How's David doing up there in Castine?

                    WILLIS
          Well he dunnit want to go overseas - oh
          no...he told them he'd keep doing it as
          long as he could stay in Maine or Vermont-

                    KATIE
               (interrupting)
          But David says if they want him to go out
          to New Mexico or California, he'll go
          back to infantry - he don't care. Long as
          he stays out here. He's not about to--

                    WILLIS
          Course he don't like working in
          recruitment anyhow's - Christ he gets
          them boys come down to to the office at
          the mall - he gets them halfway processed
          and they decide they want that delayed
          entry thing - Christ I could't do it--

                    KATIE
          Or they decide not to join up at all and--

                    WILLIS
          Well, like that one kid - he had him all
          the way through the works and then - Oh
          Christ--

                    KATIE
          His folks called David and said that the
          boy wanted out so bad -- that he'd taken
          his own life.

They all look at each other. How did this conversation get so depressing?

                    WILLIS
          Yeah well something like that gets to you
          Christ, I couldn't do it.

INT. FOWLER HOUSE - KITCHEN - DAY

Ruth is at the table, alone, dressed for rehearsal, hair done. She finishes her breakfast as she pours through the weekend's mail.

Matt in a suit, steps in to say goodbye.

                        MATT
              I'm going now.

She looks up.

                        RUTH
                   (flat)
              Okay.

                        MATT
              You ready to go back?

                        RUTH
              hm mmm.

                        MATT
                   (trying)
              You look nice.

ANGLE MATT

Who looks to Ruth for some kind of reaction. Nothing.

Matt heads out the door.

Ruth continues sorting the mail.

She stops on one piece. Seems stunned, repeatedly reading it.

THE ENVELOPE

It's from Publisher's Clearinghouse.

In oversized block letters, it reads,

FRANK FOWLER, YOU MAY HAVE ALREADY WON $10,000,000!

She stares at the piece for a long time.

Looks off. Smiles. And starts giggling. She can't stop.

The giggles quickly flow into a deep laughing fit, harder and harder as the tears rain down.

INT. MATT'S OFFICE - DAY

Matt is in his office, on the phone.

                        MATT
                   (into phone)
              Well that's totally unacceptable isn't
              it? - Well what did he say? uh huh -
              well, we can't allow that - I guess
              we're gonna have to show him how the cow
              eats the cabbage.

Janelle knocks on the door.

                        MATT
              Hold on a second.

He puts his mouth over the speaker and lowers the phone.

Nods to Janelle and she enters.

> JANELLE
> Dr. Fowler, I'm sorry. There's someone -
> Ryan Collit. His mother just brought him
> in. He doesn't have an appointment but--

> MATT
> I'm sorry but you'll have to re-schedule.

Janelle's a little taken aback.

> JANELLE
> He's Ann Collit's son. I thought. Well, you know, I
> thought you might want to -

> MATT
> (into the phone)
> I'll call back later.

He hangs up.

He gets up and grabs his jacket

> MATT
> Sorry Janelle, I'll be back at four.

> JANELLE
> (uncomfortable)
> ...o.k.

Matt leaves her standing there.

INT. DISTRICT ATTORNEY'S OFFICE - DAY

LOBBY

William Davis's secretary, REGINA, 40, sits at her desk. She is
on a call, Matt stands waiting.

> REGINA
> (hanging up)
> I'm sorry, Dr. Fowler, you just missed
> him.

> MATT
> I really need to see him. He go to lunch?

> REGINA
> That's right.

She senses something in his tone.

> REGINA
> He's across the street.

INT. MARKET ON MAIN RESTAURANT - DAY

A bustling dining room, packed with businessmen. The *nice* place in town.

It's lunch hour.

The doors open. Matt enters.

He scans the room. His eyes set on

WILLIAM DAVIS

sitting at a table with colleagues, sharing a laugh.

Matt makes his way over to the table.

Davis sees him.

                    DAVIS
          Hey, Matt.

Matt stands awkwardly, as Davis's companions look on.

                    DAVIS
               (polite)
          Have a seat.

Matt hesitates, takes a seat next to Davis.

Manages an obligatory smile to the others. The conversation resumes.

EXT. MARKET ON MAIN RESTAURANT - STREET - LATER

On the street outside the restaurant, walking.

                    DAVIS
          We're doing all we can, Matt. I promise
          you that.

                    MATT
          What can I do Bill?

                    DAVIS
          There's nothing...

Matt takes Davis's arm.

                    MATT
          It can't be manslaughter. There's got to
          be something - isn't there something you
          can find? A piece of evidence? That
          happens - doesn't that happen?

He realizes he's holding Davis's arm. He lets go.

Davis looks at Matt sympathetically.

                    DAVIS
          We really are doing everything we can,
          Matt. But I'm not going to lie to you -
          We've got no witnesses - only *Strout* - who
          claims there was a struggle - and forensic
          can't determine if there was a struggle
          because of the condition the house was in
          when Frank got there.

Matt says nothing.

They come to the corner.

Matt steps under an awning and into the shade.

Davis stops. He shifts feet a couple of times. Playing with
the change in his pocket, the way people do when they're
uncomfortable.

                    DAVIS
          Now the best thing for you to do is to
          just sit tight. We've got a whole team
          working on this case. . .

Matt nods, without looking at him.

Matt looks at Davis's hand moving the change. He becomes
hypnotized by the sound.

Davis continues talking. Matt can't hear a word of it,
though. <u>All he hears is the clinking of the coins in the
pocket.</u>

EXT. GIGI - HARBOR - DAY

Matt stands in the wheelhouse, he brings the helm about, cuts
back on the throttle and heads for the winch, the stern is
stacked with four high rows of Frank's empty traps.

Matt pulls up a string of pots. Opens the door and pulls out
a young male. He flinches and drops it. His finger goes to
his mouth.

EXT. GIGI - HARBOR - LATER

Loaded up to the gills with pots. She turns toward the
harbor.

EXT. GIGI - HARBOR - SAME

Matt at the wheelhouse heading in. His hand on the wheel,
blood trickles from his finger. He sucks on it again, reaches
down underneath his feet and pulls a Band-Aid from a box and
applies it to the finger.

EXT. "GIGI" - LATER

Matt unloads Frank's traps onto the landing.

He stops. Seems to sense something. He looks back up the gangway.

Jason sits on his bicycle watching.

The two regard each other for a moment. Then without a word Jason rides off.

INT. GRINNEL'S CROW'S NEST - DAY

Willis dries a glass. He keeps an eye on

Matt sitting at a booth at the front of the diner, silhouetted by a window. He pushes a half-eaten burger away, drains a bottle of beer. It's not the first.

THE BOOTH

Willis sets down a cup of coffee for himself. Takes a seat across from him.

They both gaze absently out the window.

INT. ROCKLAND HIGH SCHOOL - RUTH'S OFFICE - DAY

Ruth is alone at her desk, she wears headphones and is busy making notations on a sheet of manuscript paper.

There's a KNOCK on her door. She doesn't look up.

                    RUTH
             (taking off the phones)
        Yes?

There's a pause, then the door slowly opens.

Natalie takes a step in.

Ruth looks up. If she's surprised, she doesn't show it.

                    NATALIE
        I ... I hope this is okay.

Ruth says nothing. Natalie moves closer.

                    NATALIE
        I've been hoping we might be able to get
        together - to talk.

Ruth watches her as she approaches the desk. Natalie bends and cautiously extends her hand for Ruth to hold.

                    NATALIE
        I just want to tell you how ...

And in a flash Ruth SLAPS Natalie across the face with her open hand.

Natalie springs back, paralyzed with shock.

She tries to catch her breath, staring directly at Ruth.

Eyes ablaze, Ruth says nothing.

The two women look at each other for a very long time.

And finally, as if she finally somehow got the resolution she came for, head held high, Natalie turns and walks out.

EXT. STROUT & SONS CANNERY - AFTERNOON

A cyclone fence surrounds the place. A sign reads, "Strout & Sons".

It is the end of the day.

A group of workers file out, gabbing, starting to strip themselves of their smocks and hair-nets.

Tim, Frank's friend, exits with his co-workers.

He climbs into his mini pick-up, and pulls out of the lot.

A few seconds later, from outside the lot, Matt's car pulls away.

INT. SHOW & TELL - AFTERNOON - LATER

A crowded working class tavern. Video poker machines, beef jerky at the bar, Schaeffer's on tap. We're in luck. It's happy-hour.

Tim sits across from CHARLES, who is spinning a long one.

                    CHARLES
          We lost a few strings and we had a fair
          idea it was him who was doing it - so's I
          just flat out asked him "No wasn't me."
          You should of seen what he tried to pull
          last wintah. He was up to the island there
          - and he claimed our traps were in his
          part of the cove - Bobby was up to the
          tavern on the head and heard him shooting
          his mouth off about how he and his
          sternman was gonna take a bat to the old
          man & me - so's I told the old man about
          it and he says "Don't hurt my feelings
          none."He says "Go on down to the Walmart
          and buy a couple of plastic bats."
          Next day the old man walks intah the
          office at the market - near the scales -
          where he know's the son of a bitch is
          gonna come in with his catch. He's got two
          six penny nails a hammer, and the bats
          o'course, so he nails those things right
          intah the wall. The guy at the scales
          looks at him like he's nuts "Whatta ya
          doing there Ivan" he says "Just sending a
          message" and the old man walks out. I come
          in and I could see what he wrote across
          them things.

The door to the bar opens.

                    TIM
     What?

                    CHARLES
          "Here's the bats - if you got the balls."

Tim cracks up.

                    CHARLES
          Didn't touch our traps aftah that.

Tim stops mid-sentence.

Matt is passing by his table.

                    TIM
          Hey, Dr. Fowler!

Matt flinches, "surprised" to see Tim.

A FEW MINUTES LATER

Matt and Tim have moved to another booth.

Matt leans heavily on his elbows, listening to Tim.

                    TIM
          No - no, I don't even see Richard anymore.
          And he'd never tell me anything, believe
          me.

Matt takes a pull of beer.

                    MATT
          Sure, of course. I was just wondering, you
          know, maybe there was something you
          heard, through the grapevine, maybe one
          of his buddies said something ...

                    TIM
               (searching memory)
          No ...

                    MATT
          I was thinking, Richard's brothers,
          they're still working with you, right?
          They must talk.

Tim throws a nervous look over to the table where his friends
are. They're oblivious to the conversation.

He looks back to Matt, shifting in his seat.

Matt leans forward. He speaks in an intense whisper.

                         MATT
          I'm just saying, Tim, if we could find
          something, something concrete. If you
          could just ... it could be just a slip of
          the tongue ...

Tim looks into Matt's eyes, feeling the torment.

                         TIM
          I'll keep my ears open.

Matt looks at him, dissatisfied.

                         TIM
          It's funny running into you here, Dr.
          Fowler.

Matt looks at Tim blankly, then finishes his beer.

INT/EXT. MATT'S CAR - AFTERNOON - LATER

Matt drives to the end of the highway.

THE NEXT LIGHT

Matt pulls into the left-hand turn lane and signals.

There is a car in front of him. Above the license plate is a
yellow sticker that reads "Student Driver." The plate itself
is a vanity plate it says PRAY4US.

A 73 BLUE PICK-UP truck eases to a stop in the right lane, next
to Matt's car.

Matt glances over, for a moment he half expects to see Frank.

He cracks the passenger side window, for a better look.

He stares at the driver's window.

Their window rolls down.

An attractive girl with short brunette hair stares back at
Matt.

Lost in the absurdity, he doesn't look away.

The light changes.

The girl smiles sweetly and blows him a kiss, before
continuing through the light.

Matt watches her go - he smiles - as if somehow relieved.

The car behind him gives a polite toot - Matt makes the
left.

INT. SOUTH END MARKET - SAME

Ruth enters, passing the empty front register.

She strolls down an aisle, pulling some items from the shelves.

TWO MEN CHAT from the next aisle.

> MALE #1 O.S.
> yeah, man, I'd better get back to the
> grind ...

> MALE #2 O.S.
> Alright, pal ...

> MALE #1 O.S.
> Just don't steal anything.

NICK, 30'S, wearing a clerk's apron, price gun, and plastic tag that says *NICK*, rounds the end of the aisle. As he does, he spots -

RUTH, moving down the aisle toward him. He freezes.
A nervous smile. He throws a quick look to the other
aisle.

> NICK
> (a little too loudly)
> Good evening, Mrs. Fowler.

AT THE COUNTER

Ruth pulls out her purse as Nick rings her up.

> RUTH
> Oh, and a pack of Marlboro Lights.

> NICK
> Sure.

As NICK reaches up to the overhead cigarette area, he can't
help but glance past Ruth.

Ruth catches this, she turns, and sees -

RICHARD

appear from a far aisle - he makes a BEELINE FOR THE DOOR.

SHE TURNS WHITE.

As he leaves, HE LOOKS BACK.

THEIR EYES MEET - AND THEN HE'S GONE.

It's a long time before Ruth moves. Finally, she turns back to
Nick.

He looks at her, embarrassed, awaiting her reaction. She just
stares at him.

INT. FOWLER HOUSE- THE DEN - DUSK

Matt sits comfortably, feet up, beer in hand, deep into the book MORTE D'URBAN by J.F Powers.

He HEARS the front door SLAM.

He doesn't move.

Almost immediately, he hears the banging of cupboards opening and closing.

KITCHEN

Ruth is putting groceries away, ignoring, or trying to ignore, Matt who has appeared in the doorway.

She puts milk in the refrigerator and stares into it for a long time, trying to decide what to do. He can <u>feel</u> her judging him.

Finally, having resolved something in her mind, she closes the refrigerator door- revealing, taped to it, several newspaper articles on the case, gathered by her, no doubt, including one with a picture of Frank.

                    MATT
          How did it go today?

She doesn't answer.

                    MATT
          Something wrong?

She doesn't turn around.

                    RUTH
          Wrong? Like what, Matt? What could be
          wrong?

She continues "straightening up,"starts recklessly washing dishes.

Matt doesn't leave.

A plate SHATTERS in the sink.

This stops her. She stares at it, then feels his presence. She turns around.

                    RUTH
          What do you want?

He looks unsure of himself.

>   MATT
> I want to know what's going on.

>   RUTH
> Right.

>   MATT
> You're obviously upset. If there's
> something you want to talk about ...

>   RUTH
> Talk? Who, us? Oh, you mean to each other?
> What if somebody walked in? They wouldn't
> recognize us. They'd think they had the
> wrong house.

Matt takes this in. He breathes deeply.

>   MATT
> Do you want to talk or not?

>   RUTH
>   ("searching")
> Talk, talk ... oh, you must mean about our
> dead son. No, we haven't before, why
> should we bother now?

They stare at each other across the kitchen.

>   MATT
>   (slow burn)
> What can I do, Ruth?

Ruth looks at him for a long time.

>   RUTH
> Forget it, Matt. Why don't you just go ...

>   MATT
>   (building)
> What do you want from me?

>   RUTH
> I want you to stop acting like nothing's
> happened! That's what I want.

>   MATT
> Why? because I'm not bouncing off the
> walls?

>   RUTH
> No, Matt, That would require feelings. We
> don't want you to hurt yourself.

>   MATT
> Do me a favor, Ruth. You want to have a
> grieving contest, go find someone else.

He starts to turn.

> RUTH
> Yeah, I know how you grieve. Go have
> another beer.

He spins back.

> MATT
> WHAT DO YOU KNOW? WHAT? You know nothing!
> You know nothing about me. What I go
> through - every day - every lousy,
> stinking day.

> RUTH
> No, I don't know, Matt. I don't know what
> you go through, or if you go through
> anything. But that's your choice, dear,
> not mine...

> MATT
> You're goddamn right it is. My choice is
> to not scream at the world. Maybe one of
> us has to be reasonable here, did you ever
> think of that?

> RUTH
> Reasonable? Gee, Matt, I don't know about
> you, but I miss my son. I'm glad you have
> time for reason. That's what you imparted
> to Frank,that sense of reason - Oh, he
> thought you were very reasonable.

> MATT
> What the hell is that supposed to mean?

She is about to say something, but stops short.

> RUTH
> Nothing.

She turns back to the dishes.

He moves in on her, seething.

> MATT
> What are you really trying to say anyway?

She says nothing, picking up the broken plates.

> MATT
> ...that I'm the one responsible?

She drops the pieces back into the sink and exits.

THE HALL

He's fast on her heels. She heads for the bedroom.

> MATT
> Let me tell you something. Let me tell you
> something!

She throws the door closed behind her, but he bangs it open
with his palm.

                    MATT
          You got it backwards. I know what you
          think. That I was too lenient, that I let
          him get away with ...

                    RUTH
          Everything. Everything!

She exits into

THE HALL

He's right behind her.

                    MATT
          Oh, really?!? Why do you think he never
          came to you?

                    RUTH
          He wouldn't talk to me, Matt. He didn't
          trust me. You made sure of that.

THE LIVING ROOM.

                    MATT
          Why would he talk to you, Ruth? You never
          listened!

                    RUTH
          No. But you did. You were winking at him
          the whole time. You encouraged him. You
          wanted what he had. Her.

                    MATT
          You've got to be kidding...

                    RUTH
          You know it. Come on. You wanted it, and you
          couldn't get it - that's why you didn't stop him -
          so you could get your kicks through your son.
          You know that's what happened. And now you can't
          cope with it. You can't admit the truth - to me,
          or to yourself. You can't admit that he died for
          your fantasy piece of ass.

Matt, stunned, reels for a second -

And then, finally, explodes.

                    MATT
          You want to know why our son is dead,
          Ruth? He wasn't with her because of me, he
          went there because of you. Because you
          were so controlling, so overbearing, so
          angry that he was it, that he was our only
          one.

                              RUTH
          That is not true.

                              MATT
          It is! From the time he was little you
          were telling him why he was wrong.
          Everything he did was wrong. What was
          wrong with him, Ruth?

She stares at him, dumbfounded.

                              MATT
          You are so unforgiving. You are. That's
          what he said. And you're playing the same
          shit out with me. That's a horrible way to
          be! Horrible. You're bitter, Ruth. You
          can point your finger at me all you want
          -but you better take a good look at
          yourself first.

She already has, of course.

                              RUTH
                    (weary)
          I just wanted to talk about what happened,
          Matt.

                              MATT
          You expect me just to open up to you?
          Embrace you? You scare me. How can I talk
          to you? I can't even look at you.

They suddenly become aware of the DOORBELL, ringing, over and
over.

They watch each other, both reeling, both out of breath. The
DOORBELL continues.

                              MATT
                    (completely drained)
          That's probably...the police.

THE DOOR

Matt opens it. There is no cop, just Kristen Gellar, 12, a young
gymnast who'd like to compete in Hawaii.

                              KRISTEN
                    (rehearsed)
          Hi there. I'm Kristen Gellar from the
          Rockland Gymnastics Association - Today
          we're selling brand-name candy. Each
          purchase is matched by the Tandy
          corporation to help us meet our goal of
          traveling to Oahu to compete in the
          East/West conference.

Matt's in another world. He stares at her.

                         MATT
          I... um...sure. I'll take some.

                         KRISTEN
          Terrific, how many? We have a special
          today, 6 bars for ten dollars.

                         MATT
          Ok...sure.

As if by rote, Matt pulls out his wallet and hands her a ten.

                         KRISTEN
          Great! Any particular brands you like? We
          have M&M's, Goobers, Hershey's-

                         MATT
          Anything. Anything is fine ...

She finally hands him an assortment.

                         MATT
          Okay ...

He's about to close the door.

                         KRISTEN
          If you could just sign this. I have to
          give you a receipt. I'm sorry...this pen--

Matt hands her one from his pocket.

Matt waits as the girl fills out and hands him the receipt.

He closes the door before she can thank him.

THE LIVING ROOM

Ruth is curled up on the couch.

Matt stands over her, unsure of which way to go.

He stares absently into the small mountain of candy in his
hands - sets it on the coffee table.

He takes a seat at the other end of the couch.

                         MATT
          Ruth...

                         RUTH
               (softly)
          Yes?

                         MATT
          Ruth...I had no right...what I said ...no
          one, no one should ever have to hear
          that...

                    RUTH
                (barely audible)
            I'm so sorry...

He looks at her, as she starts to cry.

He moves closer to her.

                    MATT
            It's okay...

                    RUTH
            No, you're right, Matt, You are - I
            am...horrible.

                    MATT
            Please...

                    RUTH
            I don't blame you, Matt. I just...
            that girl came by. She came by the
            school, and I couldn't forgive her. I was
            so...

She lets go, crying hard.

He lifts her head onto his lap.

He reaches out, stroking her head, pulling her matted hair from
her forehead as she sobs into his lap.

                    RUTH
            I'm sorry. I have been so angry - I keep
            seeing him, Matt. I've seen him.

Matt nods, but he's not really clear.

                    MATT
                (confused)
            ...Oh I know - up in his room - Sometimes
            I swear Frank's in there - on the way home
            just now - at a stop light - for a second
            I could've--

                    RUTH
                (softly)
            Not Frank.

Matt freezes.

Then.

                    RUTH
            Richard...

She breaks into sobs.

                    RUTH
            ...and I don't know what to do.

                    MATT
          Where did you see him?

                    RUTH
          Everywhere - Downtown, and the market.   I
          saw him at South End.   He smiled at me,
          Matt - I keep running into him ... he
          smiled.

Matt still strokes her hair. But he's in another world.

INT. GRINNEL HOUSE - BASEMENT - NIGHT

The game has just started. Willis deals. Henry, Carl & Willis
pick up the old banter as if Matt had only been away on
vacation; but he can see the affection and courtesy in their
eyes.

                    WILLIS
          The name of the game is Texas Chase'em.

Henry groans.

                    WILLIS
          Is there a problem?

                    HENRY
          Why do you delude yourself with that
          crap?

                    WILLIS
          What are you talking about?

                    HENRY
          Look we're *not* in Vegas. It's five card
          draw, or seven card stud.

                    WILLIS
               (enjoying this)
          That's what I said five card draw - jacks
          to open - Carl?

                    HENRY
          Asshole.

Matt smiles. He's missed these guys.

                    CARL
          I'll open with a dollar.

                    HENRY
          Raise a buck.

The bet's to Matt. He stares at his cards for a very long
time. Willis looks to say something, when Henry hits his arm.
This stops him.

Matt looks up. He sees the patience they are all exercising for his typical indecisiveness. This bothers him.

He stares back down at his cards. Stalling, waiting for someone to bust him.

He looks up at Willis - Henry - Carl. They all sort of smile uncomfortably. He can't take it.

                    MATT
          Oh, for Christ sake say something!

This wakes them up.

                    MATT
          Quit pussy footing around me dammit! You
          just gonna let me stare at these cards
          all night!?

No one wants to make the first move.

This upsets Matt even more.

                    MATT
          O.K. fine!

He stares back down at his cards.

Finally it is Carl who speaks.

                    CARL
          There are things of which I may not speak;
          There are dreams that cannot die;
          There are thoughts that make the strong heart weak,
          And bring a pallor into the cheek,
          And a mist before the eye.
          And the words of that fatal song
          come over me like a chill:
          A boy's will is the wind's will,
          And the thoughts of youth are long, long thoughts.

Matt looks up from his cards into Carl's eyes.

The two men regard each other.

EXT. GRINNEL HOUSE - FRONT PORCH - NIGHT

The game has ended. Matt says good night to Henry and Carl, as the two of them pull out of Willis's driveway. Matt is about to leave. Just climbing into the front seat. When Willis puts a hand on his shoulder.

                    WILLIS
          Come back in for a drink.

INT. GRINNEL HOUSE- ENTRY HALL - NIGHT

Willis and Matt step back in, closing the door behind them.

                    KATIE O.S.
          Honey, are you coming to bed now?

Willis moves to the steps leading upstairs.

                    WILLIS
          Soon baby, Matt's still here.

                    KATIE O.S.
          Oh, hi Matt - Honey, would you mind
          bringing me my pills? They're downstairs
          from when the kids were here.

                    WILLIS
          I'll be right there.

INT. GRINNEL HOUSE - BASEMENT - NIGHT

A few minutes later.

Matt sits alone in the room. He gets up to examine a picture
hanging on the opposite wall. He's not particularly
interested, he's seen it a million times, he's just killing
time. The mantle over the fireplace devoted to naval memories.
A pristine version of Matt's U.S.S. CONSTELLATION cap serves
as the centerpiece.

Willis comes down from upstairs.

                    WILLIS
          She's all set - now what can I get you?

                    MATT
          I'm fine thanks.

Willis nods and takes a seat.

                    WILLIS
          - you back on the wagon?

He is.

                    WILLIS
          Sit down Matt you're making me nervous.

Matt takes a seat.

                    WILLIS
          I'm glad you came tonight.

                    MATT
          Me too.

                    WILLIS
          Boy, Carl really laid on the verse huh?

                    MATT
              (chuckling)
          yeah...yeah he did. Got me thinking
          about-

He stops himself.

                    WILLIS
          What?

                    MATT
          I don't know - sort of silly really.

                    WILLIS
          C'mon what is it?

                    MATT
          This thing with - with Frank when he was
          about <u>three</u>, I guess. We were over at my
          folk's house. Mom always liked little
          dogs - this one was a - Pekingese, I
          think. I remember hearing this yelp, and
          then a scream. Frank ran out pointing to
          his finger. I looked at it couldn't see
          <u>anything</u>. Mom said Frank must have
          "cornered the dog" and I knew she was
          probably right. We were driving home,
          and Ruth noticed Frank itching his
          arm...she pulled back his sleeve, and
          there were these two deep, bloody,
          puncture marks.....

                    WILLIS
          Why do you think he pointed to his
          finger?

Matt shakes his head.

                    MATT
                 (Searching)
          ...I <u>guess</u> he didn't want us to know.

He stares into his hands, as the memory crystallizes.

Willis looks confused, and somewhat uncomfortable.

                    WILLIS
          ...hmm

He gets up and heads to the bar.

                    MATT
                 (to himself)
          ...had to put that dog down.

Willis throws some ice in a tumbler.

                    WILLIS
          I was thinking just the other day about
          the last time Frankie was-

Matt cuts him off.

                    MATT
          His name was Frank. Not <u>Frankie</u>.

Willis looks stunned.

                    WILLIS
          ...I'm sorry Matt.

                    MATT
          I don't care...he just never liked being
          called that.

                    WILLIS
          O.K.

Matt nods. He looks away.

                    MATT
          She didn't tell me, Willis. She never
          said a word - She saw him at South End.

                    WILLIS
          ah Christ.

                    MATT
          She's seen him before. It's killing her -
          I didn't think about bail. I thought I
          wouldn't have to worry about him for
          years.

                    WILLIS
          You know what I heard? He's tending bar
          up to Old Orchard Beach.

Matt looks up.

                    WILLIS
          For a friend. Ever notice even the worst
          bastards have friends? Nobody knows him
          over there. If they do, they don't care.
          They drink what he mixes.

Willis sets a can of Moxie down in front of Matt.

                    WILLIS
               (referring to the can)
          I don't know how you drink this stuff -
          it's what drove me to beer as a child.

He sits down with his own drink.

A moment.

                    WILLIS
          I hate him, Matt. My boys went to school
          with him. He was the same then.   Know
          what he'll do? Five at the most. And
          then you'll be bumping into him all over
          again -

                    MATT
          I know.

                    WILLIS
          Remember that woman about seven years
          ago? Shot her husband and dropped him off
          the bridge in the St. George with a
          hundred pound sack of cement and said the
          whole way through it nobody helped her.
          Know where she is now? She's in Searsport
          now, a secretary. And whoever helped her,
          where the hell is he? It'd break my heart
          Matt, it would, but - you ever think about
          just - moving away?

Matt nods. Stares into his hands for a long time.

                    MATT
          Yeah, we have.

Finally, he looks up, his eyes meeting Willis's.

                    MATT
          It wouldn't matter.

THE SOUND OF A LONE FEMALE VOICE - SINGING

EXT. CAMDEN AMPHITHEATER - MAGIC HOUR

The voice is joined by another and becomes a duet. We turn to
find the voices and see we are at the foot of a small knoll.
A steeple in the distance pokes thorough the last blue husk
as the sun dies. Looking around we see an ancient gazebo -
then stairs leading up to a stone library - A boulder at the
foot of another knoll - above - descending toward us -

The girls, each holding a single candle, dressed in brightly
embroidered smocks, enter in procession singing "Jennie Mae
Mama."

The effect is beautiful and feels like a sort of quickening.
The group proceeds down the hill and blossoms into an -
AMPHITHEATER which faces the harbor. Ruth stands at the
bottom of the proscenium - her arms up - directing the choir.

The place is filled with half the town.

ANGLE MATT

Trying to take it all in. But not really present.

Suddenly he turns and leaves.

EXT. OLD ORCHARD BEACH- NIGHT

The town goes to sleep for the night. The signs & businesses
power down.

EXT. PETER'S NIGHT

The establishment's various Beer Signs & interior lights turn off.

EXT. PETER'S - NIGHT

A LARGE CHAIN OF KEYS turns the tumbler of a deadbolt lock.

Two cars are all that's left.

A WAITRESS emerges from the bar. Richard is fast on her heels. He exits, making conversation as he quickly locks the doors.

                    RICHARD
          Hey ... wait up.

                    WAITRESS
          Good night, Richard. See ya tomorrow.

She starts to walk to her car. He catches up to her, accompanying her to her car.

                    RICHARD
          You want to come over for a drink? Just a
          drink.

She stops in front of her car.

                    WAITRESS
          No, thanks. Maybe some other night.

He stands in front of his Brown Suburban, watching as the Waitress gets in her car, pulls away and leaves.

                    RICHARD
          Fuckin' bitch.

He turns and freezes.

Matt Fowler stands a few feet away, pointing an Ortgies calibre 7.65 automatic directly at Richard's face. His gloved hand grips the gun tightly.

                    RICHARD
          Dr. Fowler?

                    MATT
          Don't talk. Unlock it and get in.

                    RICHARD
          Hey...wait a minute. Let's, let's just
          calm down...

Matt COCKS the gun.

                    RICHARD
          Alright! Shit.

Richard obeys. He unlocks both doors.

Matt opens the back door, but stays planted, the gun trained on Richard.

Richard gets in the driver's seat. Matt climbs in the back.

He presses the gun's muzzle against the back of Richard's head.

>   MATT
>   Is there any one at your place?

>   RICHARD
>   (ironically)
>   Not tonight.

>   MATT
>   Good. Drive there.

Richard looks over his shoulder to back the car up.

Matt aims at his temple, but does not look at his eyes.

Richard finishes backing up and puts it into drive.

>   MATT
>   Drive slowly - don't try to get stopped.

EXT. PETER'S PARKING LOT - ALLEY

Matt can see the ocean. He uncocks the revolver.

Matt cracks the window.

Matt leans down in his seat. He transfers the gun into his left hand, removes the glove from his right, and wipes the sweat from his bare palm onto his pantleg. He puts the glove back on, gripping the gun.

Richard's brown Suburban drives down an alley adjacent to Fun Park and turns onto a deserted Main Street.

INT/EXT. BROWN SUBURBAN - NIGHT

They drive back through town, the seawall on their left hiding the beach.

On the right are the places, <u>most with their neon <u>signs off</u></u>, that do so much business in summer: the lounges and cafes and pizza houses. The street itself empty of traffic.

>   RICHARD
>   He was making it with my wife.

His voice is careful, not pleading.

Matt presses hard with the muzzle against Richard's head.

Richard flinches and moves his head forward.

Matt lowers the gun to his lap.

MATT
Don't talk.

INT/EXT. BROWN SUBURBAN - RICHARD STROUT'S DUPLEX - NIGHT

The Brown Suburban slowly pulls up to the front.

Matt leans forward. The muzzle grazing Richard's head.

MATT
Drive it to the back.

RICHARD
You wouldn't have it cocked, would you?
For when I put on the brakes.

Matt COCKS it.

MATT
It is now.

Richard tenses. He drives around the side of the building.

EXT. RICHARD STROUT'S DUPLEX - BACK YARD - NIGHT

The brown Suburban inches forward toward the garage and
brakes. The engine shuts off.

Matt keeps the cocked gun firmly trained on Richard. He gets
out and shuts the door with his hip.

MATT
All right.

Richard looks at the gun, then gets out. He moves across the
grass.

Matt follows closely behind, looking at the row of small
backyards on either side of them and scattered tall trees.

He glances from house to house. Looking for signs of one
insomniac neighbor, some man or woman sitting alone watching
the all-night channel from Boston. All is quiet.

They move up the back walk and to the side kitchen door.

Matt stands directly behind Richard as he opens the door.
It's pitch black inside the duplex.

MATT
Turn on the light.

Richard flips the wall switch.

In the light.

Matt stares at his wide back, and long reach.

INT. RICHARD STROUT'S DUPLEX - KITCHEN - NIGHT

Richard stops just inside the kitchen. Matt closes the door softly behind him.

                    MATT
          Where's your suitcase?

Richard almost turns around.

                    RICHARD
          My suitcase?

Matt grips the gun tighter, straining to keep it from trembling.

                    MATT
          Where is it?

                    RICHARD
          In the bedroom closet.

                    MATT
          That's where we're going then. When we get
          to a door you stop and turn on the light.

They cross the kitchen.

Matt can't help but glance at the sink and stove and refrigerator: no dishes in the sink or even the dish rack beside it, no grease splashings on the stove, the refrigerator clean and white.

Matt becomes momentarily preoccupied with one of Duncan's drawings - taped to its door.

                    MATT
          Wait.

Richard stops.

Matt looks conflicted. Doubt has crept into his face. For a moment he seems to have lost his resolve.

                    RICHARD O.S.
              (irritated)
          ...Jesus.

Matt looks to Richard with a renewed sense of purpose.

                    MATT
          ...keep going.

LIVING ROOM

A light flicks on. They take the hall past the living room.

Matt doesn't want to see anymore of Richard's life. But he can't help himself. He takes it all in:

Magazines and newspapers in a wicker basket,   clean ashtrays, a stereo,   CD's neatly shelved next to it.

They continue down a hallway.   Richard stops outside a door.

                    RICHARD
          There's no wall switch.

                    MATT
          Where's the light?

                    RICHARD
          By the bed.

                    MATT
          Let's go.

Richard steps into the darkness. Matt is careful to stay a pace behind. Richard leans over by the bed. Matt braces. Click. A small bedside lamp turns on.

The bed, a double one, is neatly made; the ashtray on the bedside table clean, the bureau top dustless, and no photographs; probably so the girl - who *is* she? - won't have to see Natalie in the bedroom she believes is theirs. But because Matt is a father and a husband, though never an ex-husband, he knows (and does not want to know) that this bedroom has never been theirs alone.

Richard turns around; Matt looks at his lips, his wide jaw.

                    RICHARD
          I wanted to work things out with her.
          Try to get together with her again.
          But I couldn't even talk to her.
          He was always with her.
          Dr. Fowler, I'm going to jail for it.
          I am going to jail. If I ever get out,
          I'll be an old man. Isn't that enough?

                    MATT
          You're not going to jail.
          Pack clothes for warm weather.

                    RICHARD
          What's going on? You're not gonna let me
          go!

Matt looks away. He doesn't answer.

                    RICHARD
          Dr. Fowler?

                    MATT
          You're jumping bail.

                    RICHARD
          ...Dr. Fowler.

Matt points the pistol at Richard's face. The barrel trembles a little.

Richard reaches up into his closet and pulls out two large
canvas bags. He places them on the bed. He pulls a third
bag, a small, red, woman's suitcase, Natalie's no doubt, next
to the others.

He moves to the bureau.

                    MATT
          It's the trial. We can't go through that,
          my wife and me. So you're leaving. I've
          got you a ticket. My wife keeps seeing
          you. I can't have that anymore...

                    RICHARD
          He was making it with my wife.
          I'd go pick up my kids and he'd be there.
          Sometimes he spent the night. Duncan
          told me.

He doesn't look at Matt as he speaks. He opens the top
drawer. Matt steps closer so he can see Richard's hands:
underwear and the socks rolled, the underwear folded and
stacked. Richard arranges them neatly in the suitcase. The
kitchen, the living room, the clothes. Matt is struck by
this man's sense of order, of discipline.

Matt watches the absurdity of Richard sorting clothes by
season. He even packs a small instamatic camera. He packs
the things a man accumulates and become part of him.

                    MATT
               (re: the suitcases)
          Okay, that's enough.

                    RICHARD
          I need some things from the bathroom.

                    MATT
          Alright.

THE BATHROOM

Richard steps just inside the bathroom door and stops.

                    MATT
          Keep going.

                    RICHARD
          Gotta pee.

Matt realizes Richard means to have privacy.

He pushes him into the room. Takes a step back and pulls the
door so it is only slightly ajar. He keeps his foot between
the jam and the door.

He eyes Richard's back reflected in the mirror. He can hear
him make water. He looks like he wonders about allowing this
courtesy.

Matt's glances at:

A picture on the wall outside of the bathroom: Natalie and
Richard and their two boys, in front of someone's house.
Smiling. <u>She looks happy.</u>

RICHARD

looks around the room frantically - his eyes find nothing
that will help his situation - he flushes the toilet - Matt
swings the door fully open - Richard fills a travel kit with
toiletries.

RICHARD'S BEDROOM

Richard tucks the travel kit into a bag. Matt keeps the gun
on him.

Richard closes the suitcase, and faces Matt. He looks at the
gun.

Matt moves around behind him. Now Richard is between Matt
and the lighted hall. Richard carries a canvas bag in each
hand. Matt pulls another glove from his pocket. He uses it
to turn off the bedside lamp. Richard is now silhouetted in
the doorway.

                    MATT
          Let's go.

Richard steps into the hall. Matt follows, carrying the small
suitcase in one hand, the gun in the other.

They start down the hallway. Matt turns off lights with his
elbow as they go. Past the living room into the kitchen.

                    MATT
          Wait.

Richard tenses, he stops at the kitchen door.

Matt sets the suitcase down. He uses that hand to reach into
his jacket. He pulls out a red, white, and blue piece of
paper. He drops it on the counter top. Words on the paper
read <u>AMTRAK.</u>

Matt picks up the suitcase again. He steps closer to him.
Presses the gun into Richard's back.

                    MATT
          Open the door.

Richard's reaches down and carefully turns the knob. He
slowly pulls the door open. Matt takes a step back.

                    MATT
          Get the light.

Richard reaches down and hits the switch. Click. The two men
now in silhouette.

Richard exits first. Matt close behind.

EXT. RICHARD'S DUPLEX - SAME

Matt sets the case down, reaches back and gently closes the door. They walk down the two brick steps to the lawn. <u>As they cross the lawn, Matt's eyes and ears once again alert for any sign of life</u>. <u>Nothing</u>. They reach the garage and walk to the back of the brown Suburban.

Richard drops the two bags near the rear bumper.

Matt keeps the gun steady as Richard pops open the hatch and loads the bags. Matt sets the small suitcase at Richard's feet. He reaches down and loads it last.

INT/EXT. BROWN SUBURBAN - SAME

Richard gets into the driver's seat. Matt in the back.

Richard looks up in the rear-view. For a moment, Matt connects with the desperate eyes.

                    RICHARD
          They'll catch me. They'll check passenger
          lists.

                    MATT
          I didn't use your name.

                    RICHARD
          They'll figure that out too. You think I
          wouldn't have done it myself if it was
          that easy?

Silence.

He starts it up, slides into reverse. He looks back over his shoulder as they back down the driveway. Matt averts his stare. Looking down at the gun barrel but not at the profiled face beyond it.

                    MATT
          You were alone. We've got it worked out.

                    RICHARD
          ...who's we?

Good question. Matt doesn't answer though. Richard shifts into drive.

EXT. RICHARD'S CONDO - PARKING LOT - SAME

The brown Suburban pulls out of the lot and onto the street.

INT. BROWN SUBURBAN - SAME

                    RICHARD
          There's no planes this time of night, Dr.
          Fowler.

                         MATT
          Go back through town. Then north on 73.

                         RICHARD
          The airport's South...

                         MATT
          Somebody's going to keep you for a while.
          They'll take you to the airport - turn on
          the radio. Find the game.

                         RICHARD
          It's after three -

                         MATT
          They run it again.

Matt leans back, quietly uncocking the hammer.

                         MATT
          No more talking.

Richard tries to read Matt's face in the mirror, but it's now
in shadows. Richard fumbles with the radio, surfing the AM
stations. Matt is right. The game is on.

Nomar Garciaparra hits a long drive to left with runners in scoring
position. "A cinch to collect 200 hits this season."

Richard sets his eyes on the road.

EXT. BROWN SUBURBAN - HIGHWAY 1 SOUTH - NIGHT

The brown Suburban heads away from Old Orchard, onto a small
two lane rural highway. The road is flanked on both sides by
open fields, and lonely capes. Few cars are on the road.

INT BROWN SUBURBAN/WISSCASSET BRIDGE

They come up over the high bridge over the channel: to the left
the smacking curling white at the breakwater and beyond that
the dark sea and a full moon, and down to the right the small
fishing boats bobbing at anchor in the cove.

Swirling colors from behind catch their attention.

Richard and Matt both look in the rear-view.

A state trooper's car with its gumballs flashing races up in
the distance behind them.

Matt jams the gun into Richard's ribs and slouches down.

                         MATT
                    (Trying to stay calm)
          Alright take it easy - pull over to the
          shoulder.

Matt & Richard sit tight waiting for the inevitable. The
light gains in intensity, as the cab fills with crimson.

EXT. WISCASSET BRIDGE

The cruiser tears right past them. Quickly fading into the
distance.

INT. BROWN SUBURBAN - SAME -

Matt leans back he looks shaken. Richard watches his chance
disappear.

EXT. OWL'S HEAD - NIGHT

It is almost pitch black. Only the vague outline of mountains,
hiding the moon. Then, from far off, a pair of headlights move
toward us, fighting through the thick night

INT.BROWN SUBURBAN 73 NORTH JUNCTION

Richard sees the sign for 73 North. He glances back at Matt
in the rearview mirror. He makes the turn.

EXT. OWL'S HEAD GRANGE - SAME

The Brown Suburban makes the turn.

INT. BROWN SUBURBAN - SAME

Matt & Richard check out their surroundings.

EXT. SMALL BRIDGE - NIGHT TREVETTE BRIDGE

The brown Suburban drives across a small steel bridge that
covers a salt river. The tires make a low thumping sound on
the grid.

INT. BROWN SUBURBAN - BALLYHAC ROAD (OWL'S HEAD) - NIGHT

They have left the 73 and are driving on a small rural route.
Matt leans forward, the gun rests against the top of Richard's
seat.

He looks around, trying to get a bearing.

                    MATT
          Turn around.

                    RICHARD
          Why?

                    MATT
          We missed it. Turn around. Go back and
          turn in at the last road.

EXT. RURAL ROUTE - SAME - NIGHT

Richard slows, and makes a U-turn.

His lights illuminate

PRIVATE ROAD and NO HUNTING signs.

He takes a right, onto a dirt road flanked on both sides by fir trees.

EXT.DIRT ROAD

We track with the Brown Suburban as fir trees strobe in the foreground.

INT/EXT. BROWN SUBURBAN - DIRT ROAD - SAME

                    RICHARD
          There's nothing back here Dr. Fowler? I
          don't understand why you don't just ...

                    MATT
          It's for your car. You don't think we'd
          leave it at the airport do you?

MATT WATCHES RICHARD'S LARGE, BIG KNUCKLED HANDS TIGHTEN ON THE WHEEL.

They crawl up the trail, the wheels crunching the gravel, the headlights shining into the dense woods.

The road seems endless. Richard cringes as they bounce over a bump.

Both of them eagerly peer beyond the windshield.

Finally, at a great distance, the tiny lit windows of a cabin come into view. A BLUE CHEVY PICK-UP is parked in front of the place.

                    MATT
          Stop here.

The Brown Suburban crawls to a stop. Richard keeps the engine running. Matt presses the gun hard against his neck. He straightens in his seat and looks in the rearview mirror. Matt's eyes meet his in the glass for an instant before focusing on the hair at the end of the gun barrel.

                    MATT
          Turn it off.

Richard does. The ballgame disappears, and the silence is strangely apparent. He continues to hold the wheel with both hands. He looks in the mirror.

                    RICHARD
          I'll do twenty years, Dr. Fowler-
          I'll be fifty-four years old.

                    MATT
          That's two years younger than I am.

EXT. DIRT ROAD - SAME

Matt gets out and kicks the door shut. Richard opens his door. He doesn't move. Just sits in the interior light. His face now pleading. Matt can see it in his lips.

                    MATT
          Get the bags.

                    RICHARD
                 (terrified)
          Where are we Dr. Fowler?

                    MATT
          Almost there.

Richard carefully gets out. Instinctively, he raises his hands about shoulder level. They move to the back of the Brown Suburban. Richard pops the hatch.

He pulls out the two canvas bags. He sets them on the ground. He reaches in and pulls out the small suitcase.

We hear a SCREEN DOOR slam shut. Richard looks surprised. He turns back to Matt.

                    MATT
          C'mon now.

Richard reaches down and picks up the bags. He struggles to carry all three.

Matt grabs the small suitcase from him.

                    MATT
          That way.

Richard lugs the bags toward the cabin.

We hear HEAVY CRUNCHING FOOTSTEPS OF SOMEONE APPROACHING.

Richard stops.

WILLIS APPEARS FROM DOWN THE PATH.

He nods to Matt.

                    RICHARD
          Mr. Grinnel?

                    WILLIS
          I'll get them, son.

Willis takes the bags from Richard, turns, and carries them up the long path back to the cabin.

RICHARD LOOKS SOMEWHAT RELIEVED.

He waits a moment, unsure of what to do.

Finally, he starts walking up the path after Willis.

> MATT
> Wait.

Richard stops, mid-step. He tenses, waiting.

> MATT
> You can ·carry this one.

Richard turns.

He reaches out to take the bag from Matt.

Matt keeps it at his side, and takes a step back, his gun
trained on Richard.

RICHARD CONNECTS WITH MATT'S EYES.

HE KNOWS.

RICHARD DUCKS AND TAKES ONE STEP THAT'S THE BEGINNING OF A SPRINT.

BOOM

THE GUN KICKS IN MATT'S HAND.

THE GUN'S REPORT ECHOES FOR AN ETERNITY.

MATT STANDS ABSOLUTELY STILL.

HE STILL HOLDS THE LITTLE SUITCASE.

HE LOOKS DOWN AT RICHARD STROUT SQUIRMING ON HIS BELLY. KICKING
ONE LEG BEHIND HIM, PUSHING HIMSELF FORWARD, TOWARD THE WOODS.

MATT WATCHES DISPASSIONATELY.

HE STEPS FORWARD, RAISES THE GUN AND FIRES ONE MORE SHOT.

RICHARD STOPS MOVING.

Matt stands there motionless.

We hear FOOTSTEPS.

Willis runs up to Matt.

HE STOPS AT RICHARD'S CORPSE.

> WILLIS
> (breathless)
> Matt -

The two men look into each others eyes. Matt seems to be
somewhere else. He looks back down at the body.

                        WILLIS
          This isn't what we talked about.

                        MATT
          He tried to run.

Willis looks at the gun still in Matt's hand, the little
suitcase in the other.

                        WILLIS
          We were going to wait, and take him out in
          the woods.

Matt raises his head. He looks at Willis flatly.

                        MATT
          I couldn't wait.

THE BODY -

wrapped in a BLUE TARP, is suddenly dragged away by the ATV. It
makes quite a racket.

We follow it as it scrapes along, the road back into the woods.

THE WOODS -

They have removed the body from the ATV and are now dragging it
deep into the wood. The only sound is the breaking of branches
and their continual grunting.

They stop at the top of a small knoll, panting and sweating.
Willis quietly removes a small mass of branches, revealing a
large, well-dug hole. Together, they drag the body to the edge
of the hole. Move behind it. Lift the legs, and push it in.

THE WOODS - LATER -

Willis and Matt come up from the woods. They carry Richard's
luggage. Willis drops the canvas bags into the hole. Matt
looks at the suitcase and then drops it in.

Willis takes a couple of steps away, and grabs two shovels
leaning against a small birch. He hands one to Matt.
Together, they begin filling in the hole.

SAME PLACE - LATER -

Matt holds the flashlight as Willis sprinkles leaves and
branches over the hole.

Willis freezes, as if he has heard something. Matt cuts the
light.

They hear some footsteps approaching, closer, then they see it -

A DEER

-not 30 yards distant <u>watching them</u>. A buck with a splendid rack, a deep chest, snowy white, all of him in his prime. His flag up and twitching. <u>His eyes unmoving</u>.

Then he bounds off and is gone.

THE LAKE WOODS - LATER -

They walk through the woods. The light on the ground. They both look up through the trees where they end at the lake.

Neither of them speak, only the sounds of their heavy breathing and clumsy strides through the low brush and over fallen branches.

EXT. BOW LAKE -

Wide and dark, lapping softly at the bank, a small island near it's middle, with black, tall evergreens.

Matt, gun in hand, takes two steps back, he strides with the throw and goes to one knee as he follows through. The dark shapeless object arcing downward, splashing.

THE DIRT ROAD, NEAR THE BROWN SUBURBAN.

INT/EXT. BROWN SUBURBAN - TREVETT SWINGBRIDGE - NIGHT

Matt in the brown Suburban, is stopped behind the wooden guard arm, Willis in his own car behind. The swing bridge is open for the 5:00A.M. fishing boats. The operator uses his long metal tool, the bridge swings back around. The arm rises.

MATT

Seems somewhere else.

WILLIS

                    WILLIS
                  (angry)
              C'mon go Matt.

Matt drives the Brown Suburban over the bridge. The operator gives him a friendly nod. Waves to Willis in the Ford.

EXT. WISCASSET BRIDGE - PRE-DAWN

Willis's truck & Richard's SUV travel toward us, away from Wiscasset. On their way to Cheesy Town Island.

INT. FORD - OLD ORCHARD STATION - PRE-DAWN

Willis watches out his windshield as the Brown Suburban parks in the station's lot.

Matt gets out of the brown Suburban and locks the driver's door. He walks to the Ford, and gets in the passenger side. They drive off.

INT/EXT. WISSCASSET BRIDGE - SAME

Willis's car moves slowly over the channel bridge, back to
Wiscasset.

Matt rolls down his window. <u>He tosses Richard's keys over the side of
the bridge</u>. The trim shapes of lobster boats and small craft anchored
in the harbor below, look like old toys in a bathtub.

He rolls up the window as the car continues across.

Both men silent, lost in thought, staring out the windshield at
the road ahead.

>   WILLIS
>   (softly)
>   What time is it?

Matt checks his watch.

>   MATT
>   Ten to six. We lost an hour. Sorry.

Willis's jaw tightens.

>   WILLIS
>   (almost losing his temper)
>   Yep...high tide. Can't stop people from
>   fish'in Matt - <u>Fuck'in bridge!</u>

Matt looks over at Willis.

>   MATT
>   I'm sorry Willis.

Willis looks at Matt. He knows. Eyes back to the road.

>   WILLIS
>   (forced calm)
>   Stopped into his little shed there once -
>   place *reeked*...the guy's *spilled* more
>   whiskey than we've ever drunk. Just pray
>   he's already three sheets to the wind.

Matt doesn't reply.

>   WILLIS
>   Katie's pill will be wearing off soon.

INT/EXT.FORD - MAIN STREET ROCKLAND - DAWN

They drive down the empty streets of a sleeping Rockland.

Past the -

<u>MEN OF ROCKLAND CIVIL WAR MEMORIAL</u>, TWO SENTRIES STAND GUARD.

Past -

ROCKLAND HIGH SCHOOL.

Past -

ROCKLAND POLICE DEPT.

Past -

YVONNE'S SPECIALTY SHOPPE

Something catches Matt's attention in the store front.

The mannequins in the window. They seem to be staring at him.

STROUT & SONS CANNERY

Past -

CAMDEN ARCH

EXT. SIDE STREET - MATT'S NEIGHBORHOOD - DAWN

The Ford pulls up to the curb. Matt gets out.

Willis drives away.

Matt starts walking.

EXT.FOWLER STREET - SAME

The STREET LIGHTS suddenly turn off.

The world is waking up now.

EXT. FOWLER STREET - SAME

In the distance, Matt can see his house.

The birds all seem to wake at once.

Matt gazes up into the trees overhead, the first light just
kissing their branches, the sky now a husky blue. The
surrounding houses with the windows still dark, asleep.

He picks up his pace.

INT. FOWLER HOUSE - BARN - SAME

Matt enters.

THE LAUNDRY ROOM - SAME

He removes his tennis shoes, his pants, he starts unbuttoning
his shirt. Now in his T-shirt and boxers, he examines his
clothes and shoes carefully, before putting them into the
washer - He pours detergent inside - and starts the cycle.
He steps to a little sink and washes up.

THE DINING ROOM -

The light has been left on, he kills it and heads upstairs.

UPSTAIRS - SAME

Matt slowly walks down the hall, to

THE BEDROOM - SAME

And stands in the doorway. He pauses, seeing only

the orange ember of Ruth's cigarette, in the dark.

> RUTH
> (unseen)
> Did you do it?

He doesn't answer. He walks in and comes to bed, climbing in as
Ruth moves over.

> RUTH
> Are you all right?

He lies down. HE FACES THE WINDOW, AWAY FROM HER.

She is on her side, she props herself up on her elbow -
watching him.

He waits a long time before speaking.

> MATT
> There was a picture with Natalie and the
> boys hanging on his wall -

Ruth looks at him strangely.

> RUTH
> (gently)
> ...what is it, Matt?

> MATT
> - the way she was *smiling.*

> RUTH
> What?

> MATT
> I don't know -

Ruth looks at the back of Matt's head.

> RUTH
> Matt?

He doesn't move. He says nothing else. She continues to stare at him.

Uncertainty beginning to form on her face. She looks lost. If only things could be as they were.

Then.

> RUTH
> What am I thinking - you must be hungry.

She waits for a response, but gets none. She gets out of bed, leaves the room and heads downstairs.

A LONG EMPTY HALLWAY.

WE HEAR RUTH downstairs in the kitchen.

> RUTH O.S.
> Matt?

Matt just lies there, in another world.

> RUTH
> Matt dear, do you want coffee?

He doesn't respond. Instead he looks at his finger.

The bandage wet from washing up.

He slides it off easily, like an oversized ring.

The skin has healed.

LATER NOW -

Sun light creeps in through the curtains, onto Matt's face.

Ruth lies sleeping on his chest.

A breakfast tray at his bedside, which he hasn't touched.

Matt is wide awake. He stares at the ceiling. Reliving it.

His eyes full of an unspeakable sadness.

The lids heavy. If only he could sleep.

But he won't. Not today.

There is a small crack in the ceiling.

He'll have to fix that.

> BLACK

> - THE FAINT SOUNDS OF FENWAY PARK FADE UP -

> THE END